THE COMIC COLLECTION

A GERRY ANDERSON PRODUCTION

THUNDERBIRDS™

THUNDERBIRD 2
2

CLASSIC COMICS

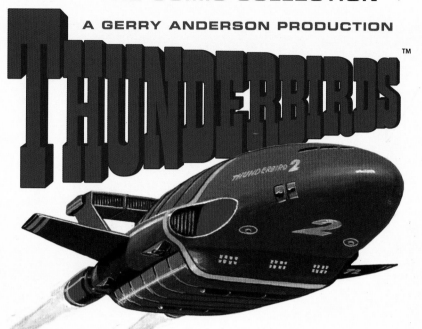

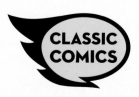

EGMONT

EGMONT

This volume first published in Great Britain 2014 by Egmont UK Limited
The Yellow Building, 1 Nicholas Road, London W11 4AN
Thunderbirds ™ and © ITC Entertainment Group Limited 1964, 1999 and 2014.
Licensed by ITV Ventures Limited. All rights reserved.

A GERRY ANDERSON PRODUCTION

Cover illustration by Graham Bleathman

ISBN 978 1 4052 7261 2
56508/1
Printed in Malaysia.

Please note: Some of the comic strips used in this collection
are exceedingly rare, so the print quality may vary.

Egmont is passionate about helping to preserve the world's remaining ancient forests.
We only use paper from legal and sustainable forest sources.

This book is made from paper certified by the Forest Stewardship Council® (FSC®),
an organisation dedicated to promoting responsible management of forest resources.
For more information on the FSC, please visit www.fsc.org. To learn more about
Egmont's sustainable paper policy, please visit www.egmont.co.uk/ethical

Stay safe online. Egmont is not responsible for content hosted by third parties.

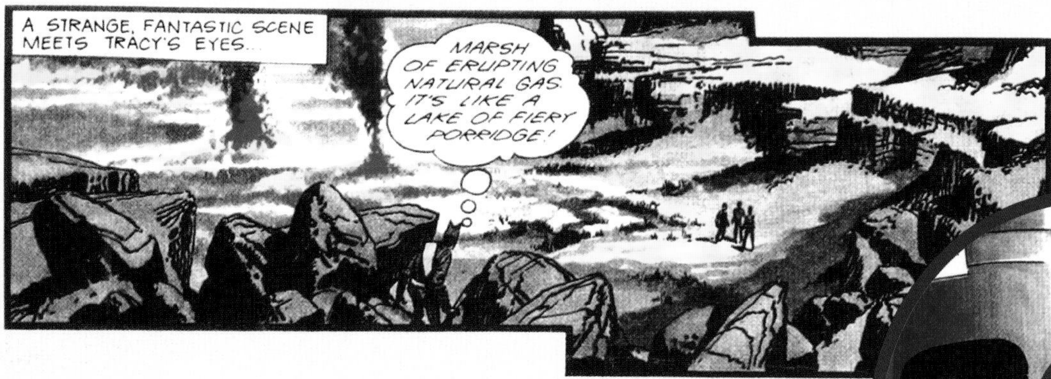
A STRANGE, FANTASTIC SCENE MEETS TRACY'S EYES...
MARSH OF ERUPTING NATURAL GAS. IT'S LIKE A LAKE OF FIERY PORRIDGE!

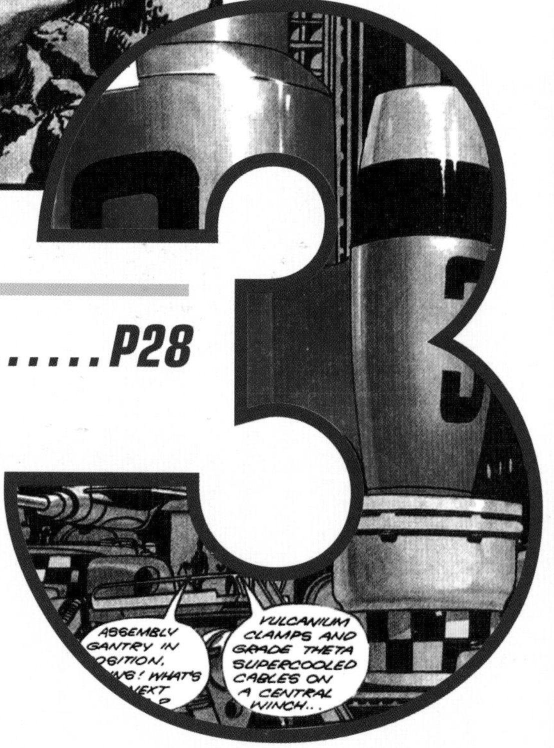
ASSEMBLY GANTRY IN
VULCANIUM CLAMPS AND GRADE THETA SUPERCOOLED CABLES ON A CENTRAL WINCH...

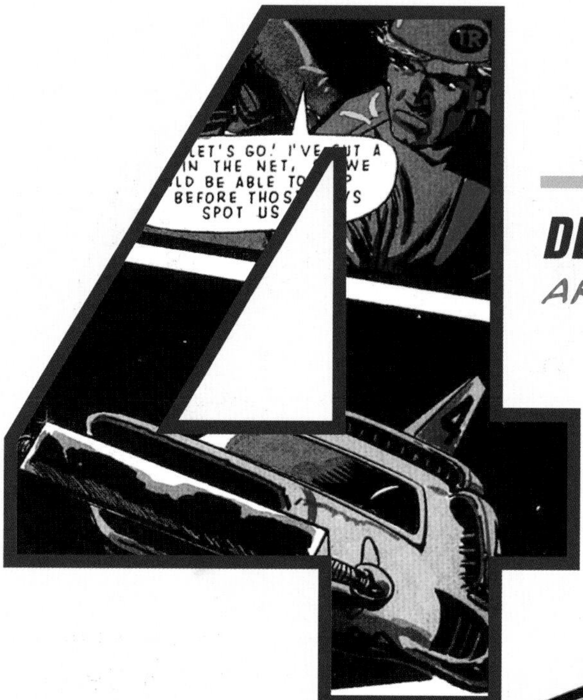

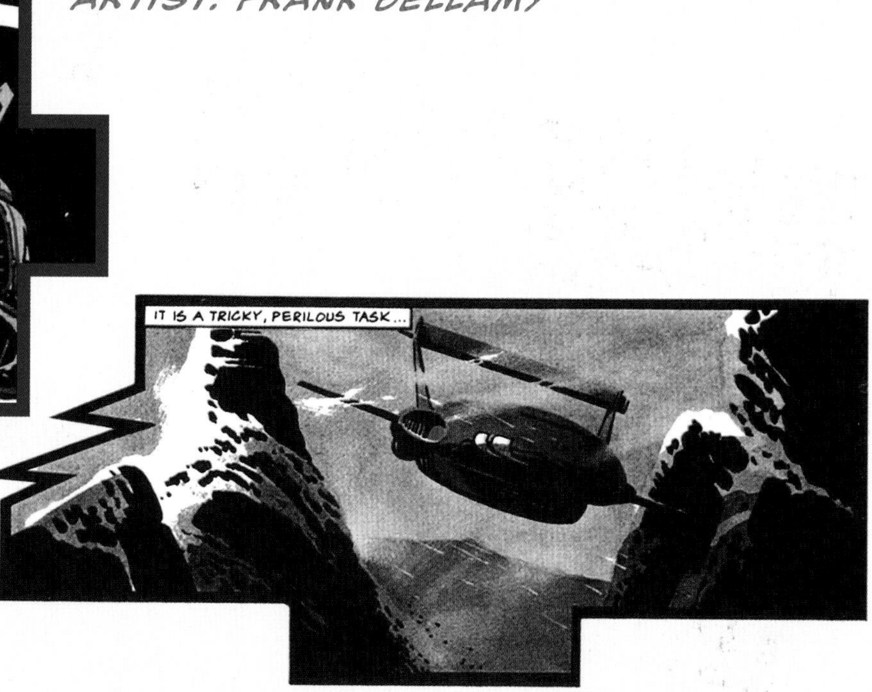
IT IS A TRICKY, PERILOUS TASK...

Part 1 - dateline 24 February 2068

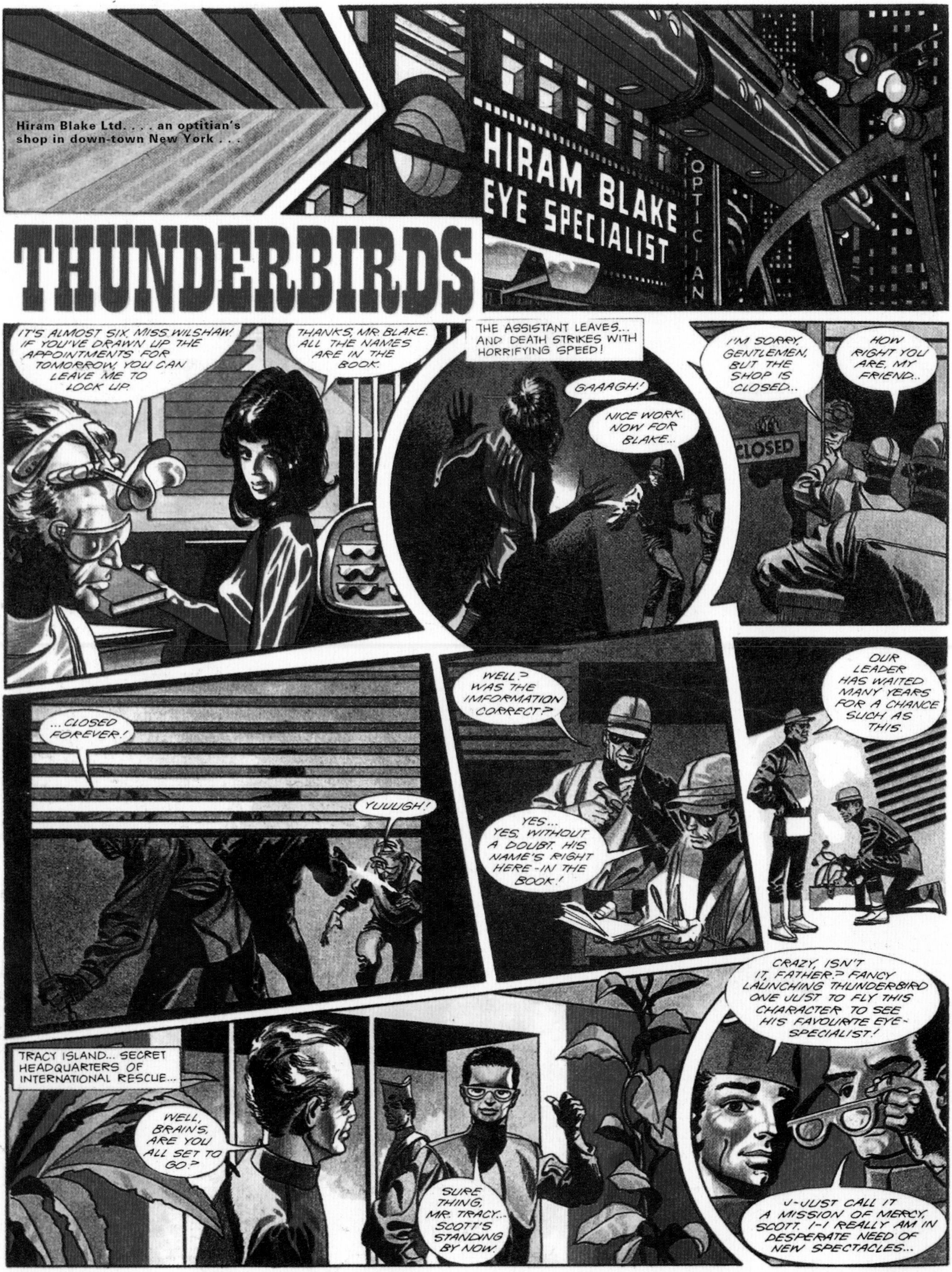
Hiram Blake Ltd. . . . an optitian's shop in down-town New York . . .
HIRAM BLAKE EYE SPECIALIST
OPTICIAN
THUNDERBIRDS
IT'S ALMOST SIX, MISS WILSHAW. IF YOU'VE DRAWN UP THE APPOINTMENTS FOR TOMORROW, YOU CAN LEAVE ME TO LOCK UP.
THANKS, MR. BLAKE. ALL THE NAMES ARE IN THE BOOK.
THE ASSISTANT LEAVES... AND DEATH STRIKES WITH HORRIFYING SPEED!
GAAAGH!
NICE WORK. NOW FOR BLAKE...
I'M SORRY, GENTLEMEN, BUT THE SHOP IS CLOSED...
HOW RIGHT YOU ARE, MY FRIEND...
CLOSED
...CLOSED FOREVER!
YUUUGH!
WELL? WAS THE INFORMATION CORRECT?
YES... YES, WITHOUT A DOUBT. HIS NAME'S RIGHT HERE - IN THE BOOK!
OUR LEADER HAS WAITED MANY YEARS FOR A CHANCE SUCH AS THIS.
TRACY ISLAND... SECRET HEADQUARTERS OF INTERNATIONAL RESCUE...
WELL, BRAINS, ARE YOU ALL SET TO GO?
SURE THING, MR. TRACY... SCOTT'S STANDING BY NOW.
CRAZY, ISN'T IT, FATHER? FANCY LAUNCHING THUNDERBIRD ONE JUST TO FLY THIS CHARACTER TO SEE HIS FAVOURITE EYE-SPECIALIST!
J-JUST CALL IT A MISSION OF MERCY, SCOTT. I-I REALLY AM IN DESPERATE NEED OF NEW SPECTACLES...

Artist: Frank Bellamy

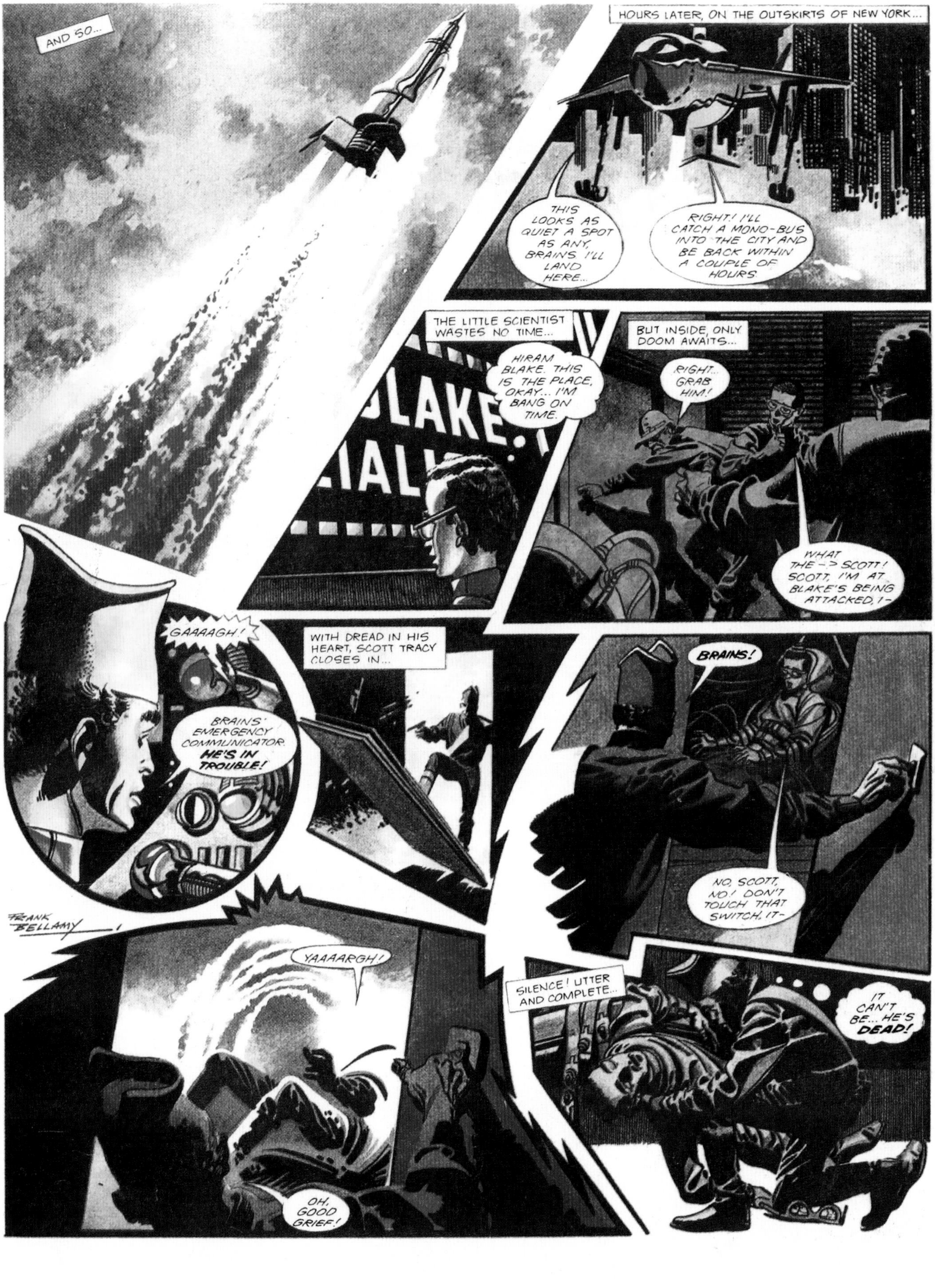
AND SO...
HOURS LATER, ON THE OUTSKIRTS OF NEW YORK...
THIS LOOKS AS QUIET A SPOT AS ANY, BRAINS. I'LL LAND HERE...
RIGHT! I'LL CATCH A MONO-BUS INTO THE CITY AND BE BACK WITHIN A COUPLE OF HOURS.
THE LITTLE SCIENTIST WASTES NO TIME...
HIRAM BLAKE. THIS IS THE PLACE, OKAY... I'M BANG ON TIME.
BUT INSIDE, ONLY DOOM AWAITS...
RIGHT... GRAB HIM!
WHAT THE--> SCOTT! SCOTT, I'M AT BLAKE'S BEING ATTACKED, !-
GAAAAGH!
BRAINS' EMERGENCY COMMUNICATOR. HE'S IN TROUBLE!
WITH DREAD IN HIS HEART, SCOTT TRACY CLOSES IN...
BRAINS!
NO, SCOTT, NO! DON'T TOUCH THAT SWITCH, IT-
FRANK BELLAMY
YAAAARGH!
OH, GOOD GRIEF!
SILENCE! UTTER AND COMPLETE...
IT CAN'T BE... HE'S DEAD!

Part 2 - dateline 02 March 2068

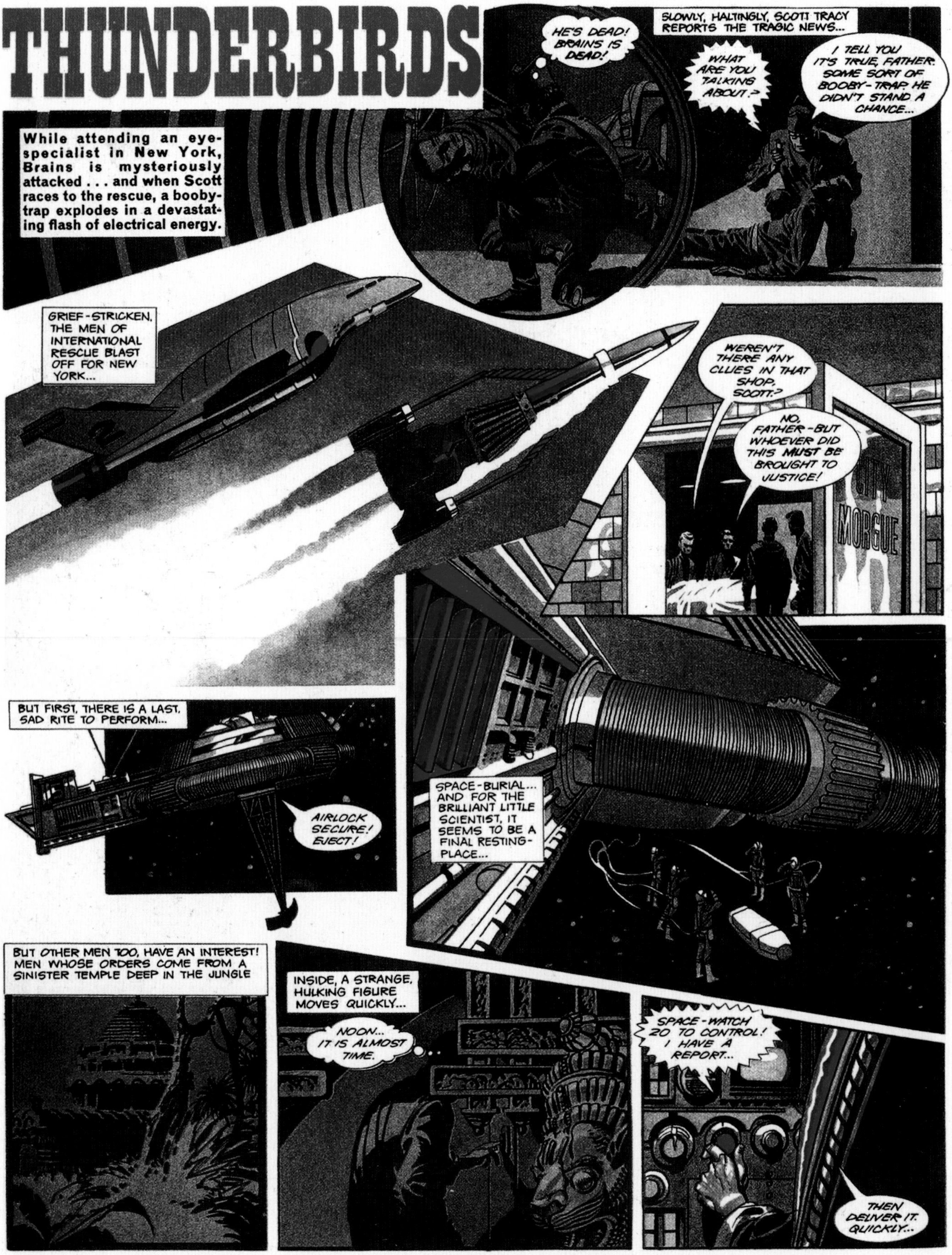
THUNDERBIRDS
While attending an eye-specialist in New York, Brains is mysteriously attacked . . . and when Scott races to the rescue, a booby-trap explodes in a devastating flash of electrical energy.
HE'S DEAD! BRAINS IS DEAD!
SLOWLY, HALTINGLY, SCOTT TRACY REPORTS THE TRAGIC NEWS...
WHAT ARE YOU TALKING ABOUT?
I TELL YOU IT'S TRUE, FATHER. SOME SORT OF BOOBY-TRAP. HE DIDN'T STAND A CHANCE...
GRIEF-STRICKEN, THE MEN OF INTERNATIONAL RESCUE BLAST OFF FOR NEW YORK...
WEREN'T THERE ANY CLUES IN THAT SHOP, SCOTT?
NO, FATHER-BUT WHOEVER DID THIS MUST BE BROUGHT TO JUSTICE!
CITY MORGUE
BUT FIRST, THERE IS A LAST, SAD RITE TO PERFORM...
AIRLOCK SECURE! EJECT!
SPACE-BURIAL... AND FOR THE BRILLIANT LITTLE SCIENTIST, IT SEEMS TO BE A FINAL RESTING-PLACE...
BUT OTHER MEN TOO, HAVE AN INTEREST! MEN WHOSE ORDERS COME FROM A SINISTER TEMPLE DEEP IN THE JUNGLE
INSIDE, A STRANGE, HULKING FIGURE MOVES QUICKLY...
NOON... IT IS ALMOST TIME.
SPACE-WATCH 20 TO CONTROL! I HAVE A REPORT...
THEN DELIVER IT. QUICKLY...

Artist: Frank Bellamy

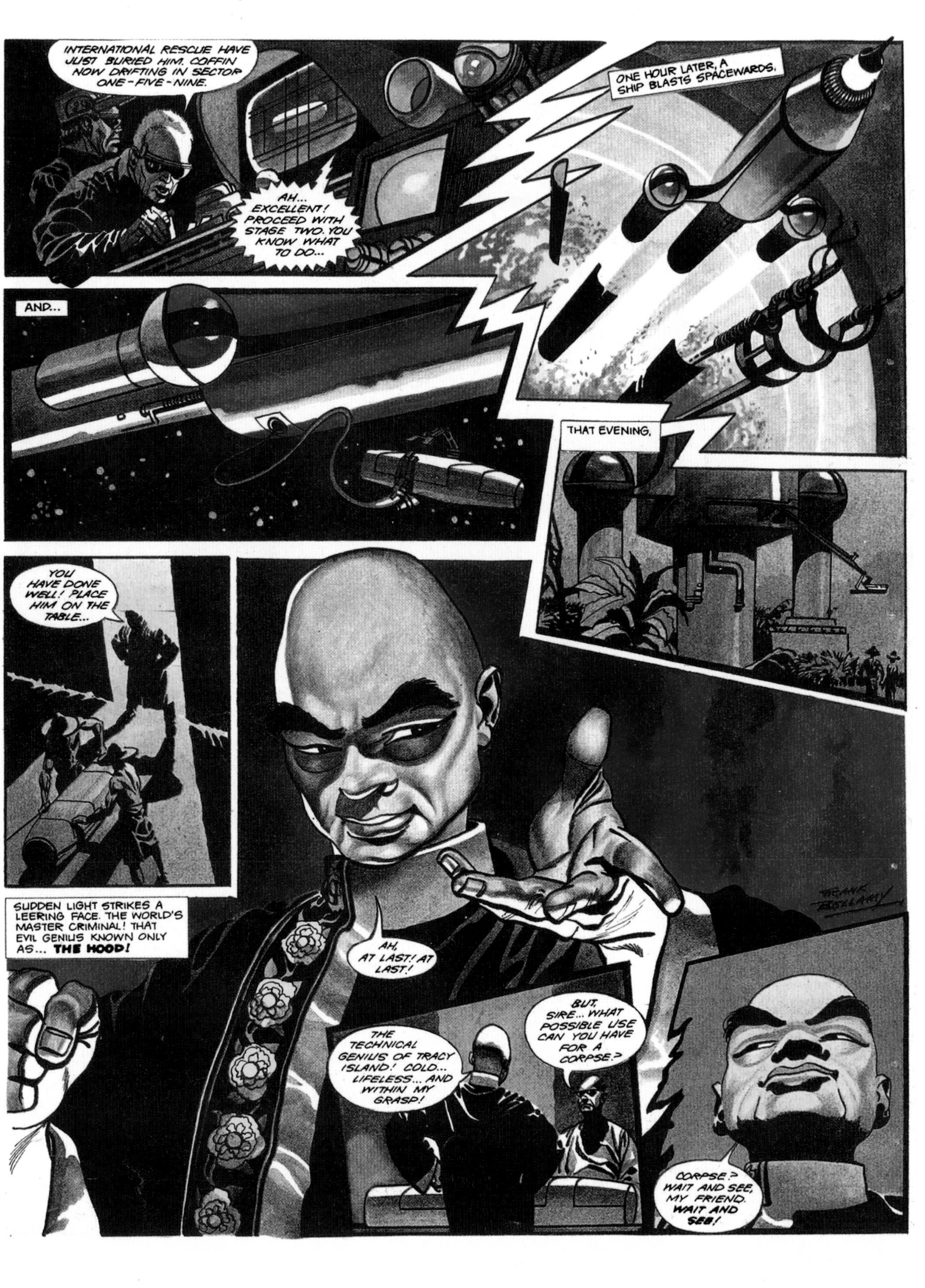
INTERNATIONAL RESCUE HAVE JUST BURIED HIM. COFFIN NOW DRIFTING IN SECTOR ONE-FIVE-NINE.
AH... EXCELLENT! PROCEED WITH STAGE TWO. YOU KNOW WHAT TO DO...
ONE HOUR LATER, A SHIP BLASTS SPACEWARDS.
AND...
THAT EVENING,
YOU HAVE DONE WELL! PLACE HIM ON THE TABLE...
SUDDEN LIGHT STRIKES A LEERING FACE. THE WORLD'S MASTER CRIMINAL! THAT EVIL GENIUS KNOWN ONLY AS... THE HOOD!
AH, AT LAST! AT LAST!
THE TECHNICAL GENIUS OF TRACY ISLAND! COLD... LIFELESS... AND WITHIN MY GRASP!
BUT, SIRE... WHAT POSSIBLE USE CAN YOU HAVE FOR A CORPSE?
CORPSE? WAIT AND SEE, MY FRIEND. WAIT AND SEE!

Part 3 - dateline 09 March 2068

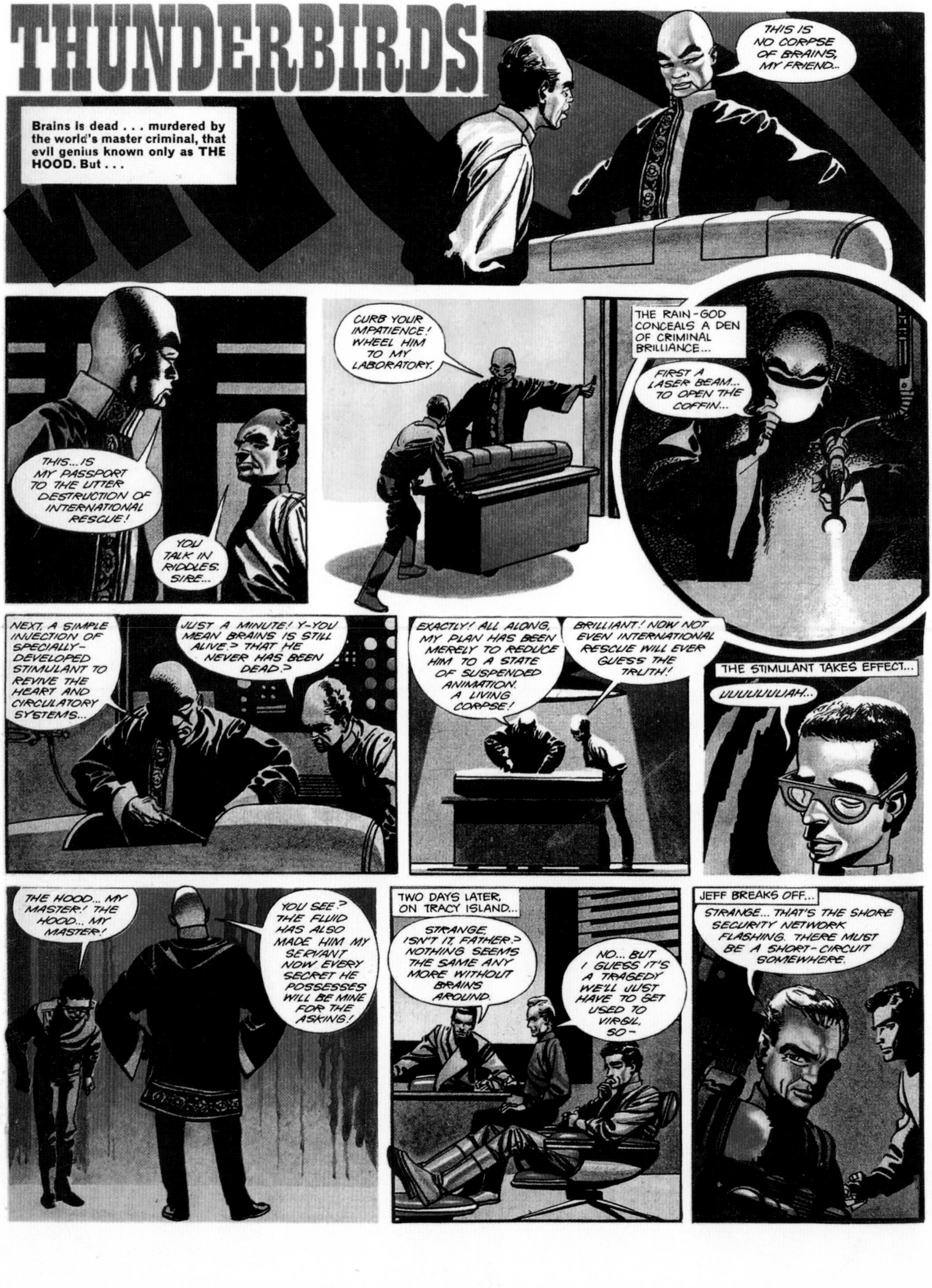
THUNDERBIRDS
Brains is dead . . . murdered by the world's master criminal, that evil genius known only as THE HOOD. But . . .
THIS IS NO CORPSE OF BRAINS, MY FRIEND...
THIS... IS MY PASSPORT TO THE UTTER DESTRUCTION OF INTERNATIONAL RESCUE!
YOU TALK IN RIDDLES, SIRE...
CURB YOUR IMPATIENCE! WHEEL HIM TO MY LABORATORY.
THE RAIN-GOD CONCEALS A DEN OF CRIMINAL BRILLIANCE...
FIRST A LASER BEAM... TO OPEN THE COFFIN...
NEXT, A SIMPLE INJECTION OF SPECIALLY-DEVELOPED STIMULANT TO REVIVE THE HEART AND CIRCULATORY SYSTEMS...
JUST A MINUTE! Y-YOU MEAN BRAINS IS STILL ALIVE? THAT HE NEVER HAS BEEN DEAD?
EXACTLY! ALL ALONG, MY PLAN HAS BEEN MERELY TO REDUCE HIM TO A STATE OF SUSPENDED ANIMATION. A LIVING CORPSE!
BRILLIANT! NOW NOT EVEN INTERNATIONAL RESCUE WILL EVER GUESS THE TRUTH!
THE STIMULANT TAKES EFFECT...
UUUUUUUAH...
THE HOOD... MY MASTER! THE HOOD... MY MASTER!
YOU SEE? THE FLUID HAS ALSO MADE HIM MY SERVANT NOW EVERY SECRET HE POSSESSES WILL BE MINE FOR THE ASKING!
TWO DAYS LATER, ON TRACY ISLAND...
STRANGE, ISN'T IT, FATHER? NOTHING SEEMS THE SAME ANY MORE WITHOUT BRAINS AROUND.
NO... BUT I GUESS IT'S A TRAGEDY WE'LL JUST HAVE TO GET USED TO VIRGIL. SO—
JEFF BREAKS OFF...
STRANGE... THAT'S THE SHORE SECURITY NETWORK FLASHING. THERE MUST BE A SHORT-CIRCUIT SOMEWHERE.

Artist: Frank Bellamy

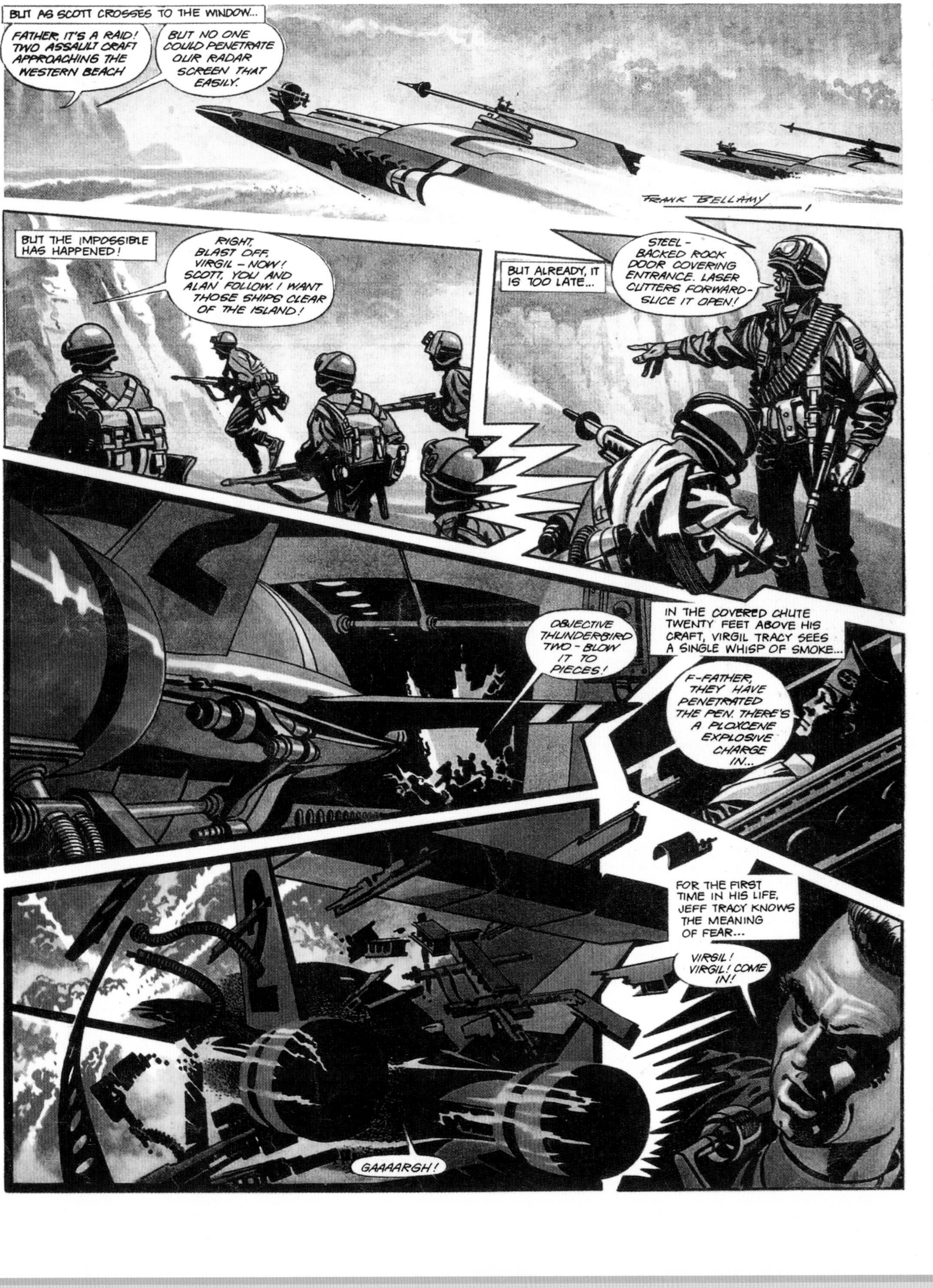
BUT AS SCOTT CROSSES TO THE WINDOW...
FATHER, IT'S A RAID! TWO ASSAULT CRAFT APPROACHING THE WESTERN BEACH
BUT NO ONE COULD PENETRATE OUR RADAR SCREEN THAT EASILY.
FRANK BELLAMY
BUT THE IMPOSSIBLE HAS HAPPENED!
RIGHT, BLAST OFF, VIRGIL – NOW! SCOTT, YOU AND ALAN FOLLOW. I WANT THOSE SHIPS CLEAR OF THE ISLAND!
BUT ALREADY, IT IS TOO LATE...
STEEL-BACKED ROCK DOOR COVERING ENTRANCE. LASER CUTTERS FORWARD– SLICE IT OPEN!
OBJECTIVE THUNDERBIRD TWO – BLOW IT TO PIECES!
IN THE COVERED CHUTE TWENTY FEET ABOVE HIS CRAFT, VIRGIL TRACY SEES A SINGLE WHISP OF SMOKE...
F-FATHER, THEY HAVE PENETRATED THE PEN. THERE'S A PLOXCENE EXPLOSIVE CHARGE IN...
FOR THE FIRST TIME IN HIS LIFE, JEFF TRACY KNOWS THE MEANING OF FEAR...
VIRGIL! VIRGIL! COME IN!
GAAAARGH!

Part 4 - dateline 16 March 2068

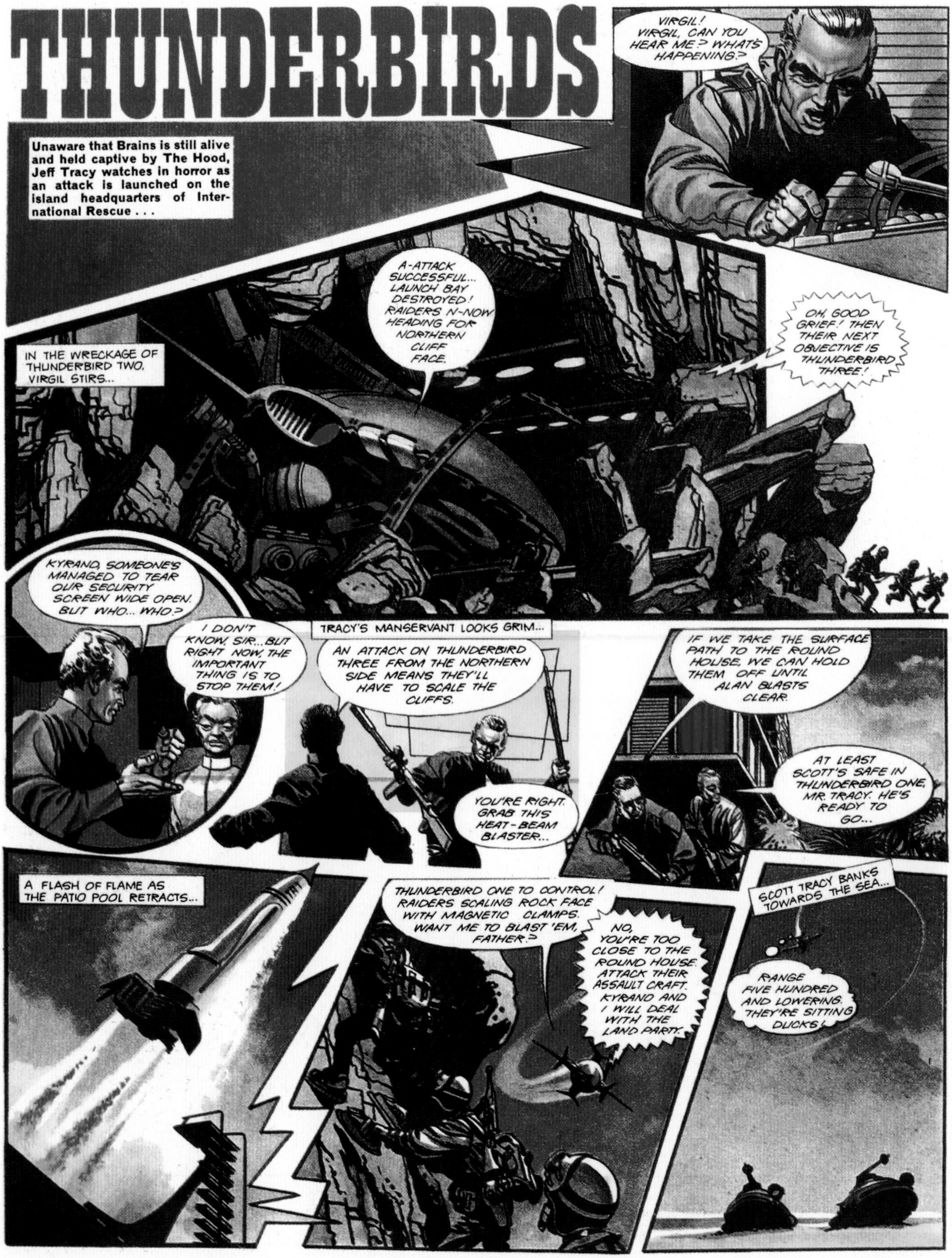
THUNDERBIRDS
VIRGIL! VIRGIL, CAN YOU HEAR ME? WHAT'S HAPPENING?
Unaware that Brains is still alive and held captive by The Hood, Jeff Tracy watches in horror as an attack is launched on the island headquarters of International Rescue . . .
IN THE WRECKAGE OF THUNDERBIRD TWO, VIRGIL STIRS...
A-ATTACK SUCCESSFUL... LAUNCH BAY DESTROYED! RAIDERS N-NOW HEADING FOR NORTHERN CLIFF FACE.
OH, GOOD GRIEF! THEN THEIR NEXT OBJECTIVE IS THUNDERBIRD THREE!
KYRANO, SOMEONE'S MANAGED TO TEAR OUR SECURITY SCREEN WIDE OPEN. BUT WHO... WHO?
I DON'T KNOW, SIR... BUT RIGHT NOW, THE IMPORTANT THING IS TO STOP THEM!
TRACY'S MANSERVANT LOOKS GRIM...
AN ATTACK ON THUNDERBIRD THREE FROM THE NORTHERN SIDE MEANS THEY'LL HAVE TO SCALE THE CLIFFS.
YOU'RE RIGHT. GRAB THIS HEAT-BEAM BLASTER...
IF WE TAKE THE SURFACE PATH TO THE ROUND HOUSE, WE CAN HOLD THEM OFF UNTIL ALAN BLASTS CLEAR.
AT LEAST SCOTT'S SAFE IN THUNDERBIRD ONE, MR. TRACY. HE'S READY TO GO...
A FLASH OF FLAME AS THE PATIO POOL RETRACTS...
THUNDERBIRD ONE TO CONTROL! RAIDERS SCALING ROCK FACE WITH MAGNETIC CLAMPS. WANT ME TO BLAST 'EM, FATHER?
NO, YOU'RE TOO CLOSE TO THE ROUND HOUSE. ATTACK THEIR ASSAULT CRAFT. KYRANO AND I WILL DEAL WITH THE LAND PARTY.
SCOTT TRACY BANKS TOWARDS THE SEA...
RANGE FIVE HUNDRED AND LOWERING. THEY'RE SITTING DUCKS!

Artist: Frank Bellamy

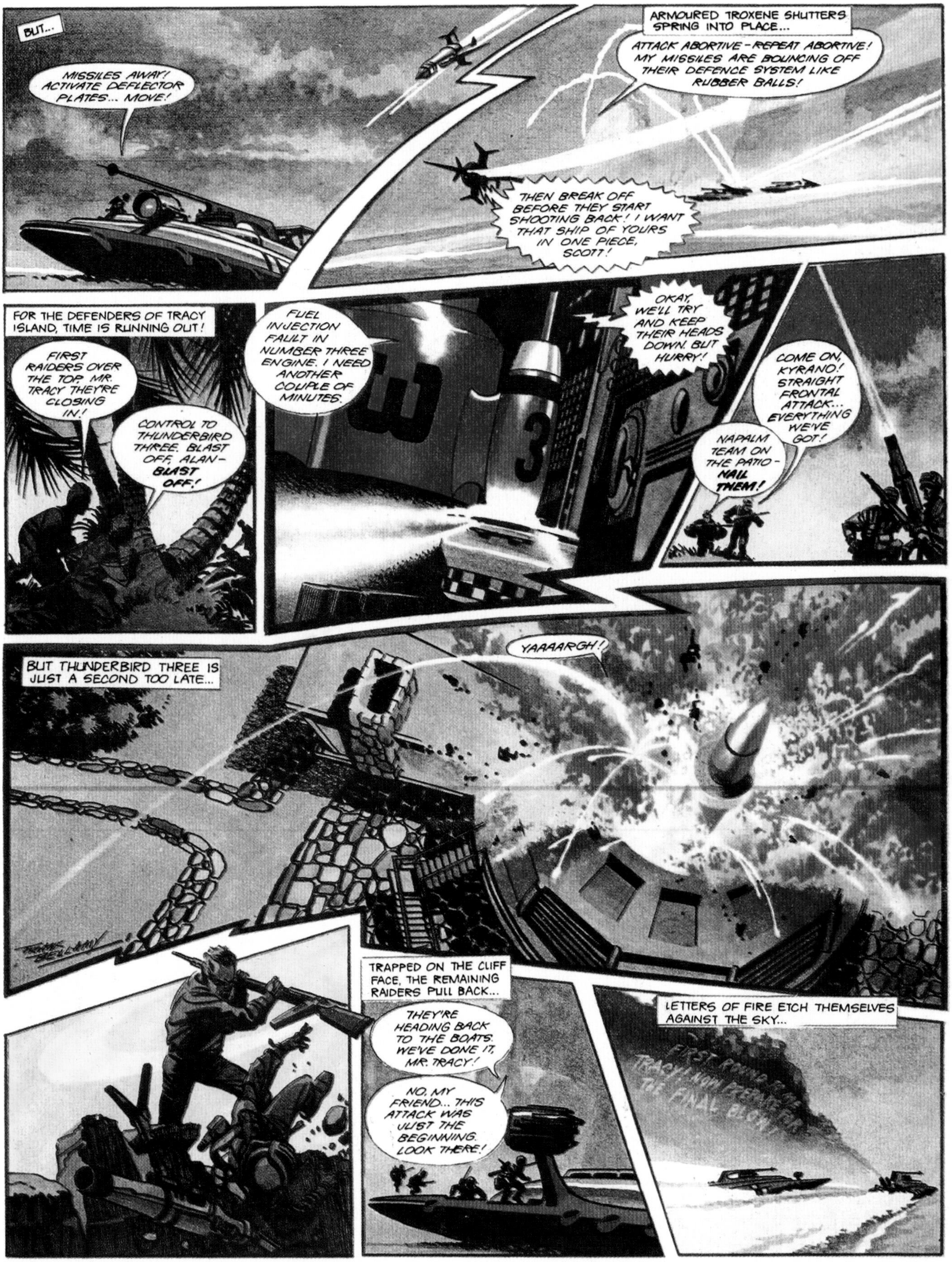
BUT...
MISSILES AWAY! ACTIVATE DEFLECTOR PLATES... MOVE!
ARMOURED TROXENE SHUTTERS SPRING INTO PLACE...
ATTACK ABORTIVE - REPEAT ABORTIVE! MY MISSILES ARE BOUNCING OFF THEIR DEFENCE SYSTEM LIKE RUBBER BALLS!
THEN BREAK OFF BEFORE THEY START SHOOTING BACK! I WANT THAT SHIP OF YOURS IN ONE PIECE, SCOTT!
FOR THE DEFENDERS OF TRACY ISLAND, TIME IS RUNNING OUT!
FIRST RAIDERS OVER THE TOP, MR. TRACY. THEY'RE CLOSING IN!
CONTROL TO THUNDERBIRD THREE. BLAST OFF, ALAN - BLAST OFF!
FUEL INJECTION FAULT IN NUMBER THREE ENGINE. I NEED ANOTHER COUPLE OF MINUTES.
OKAY, WE'LL TRY AND KEEP THEIR HEADS DOWN. BUT HURRY!
COME ON, KYRANO! STRAIGHT FRONTAL ATTACK... EVERYTHING WE'VE GOT!
NAPALM TEAM ON THE PATIO - NAIL THEM!
BUT THUNDERBIRD THREE IS JUST A SECOND TOO LATE...
YAAAARGH!
TRAPPED ON THE CLIFF FACE, THE REMAINING RAIDERS PULL BACK...
THEY'RE HEADING BACK TO THE BOATS. WE'VE DONE IT, MR. TRACY!
NO, MY FRIEND... THIS ATTACK WAS JUST THE BEGINNING. LOOK THERE!
LETTERS OF FIRE ETCH THEMSELVES AGAINST THE SKY...

Part 5 - dateline 23 March 2068

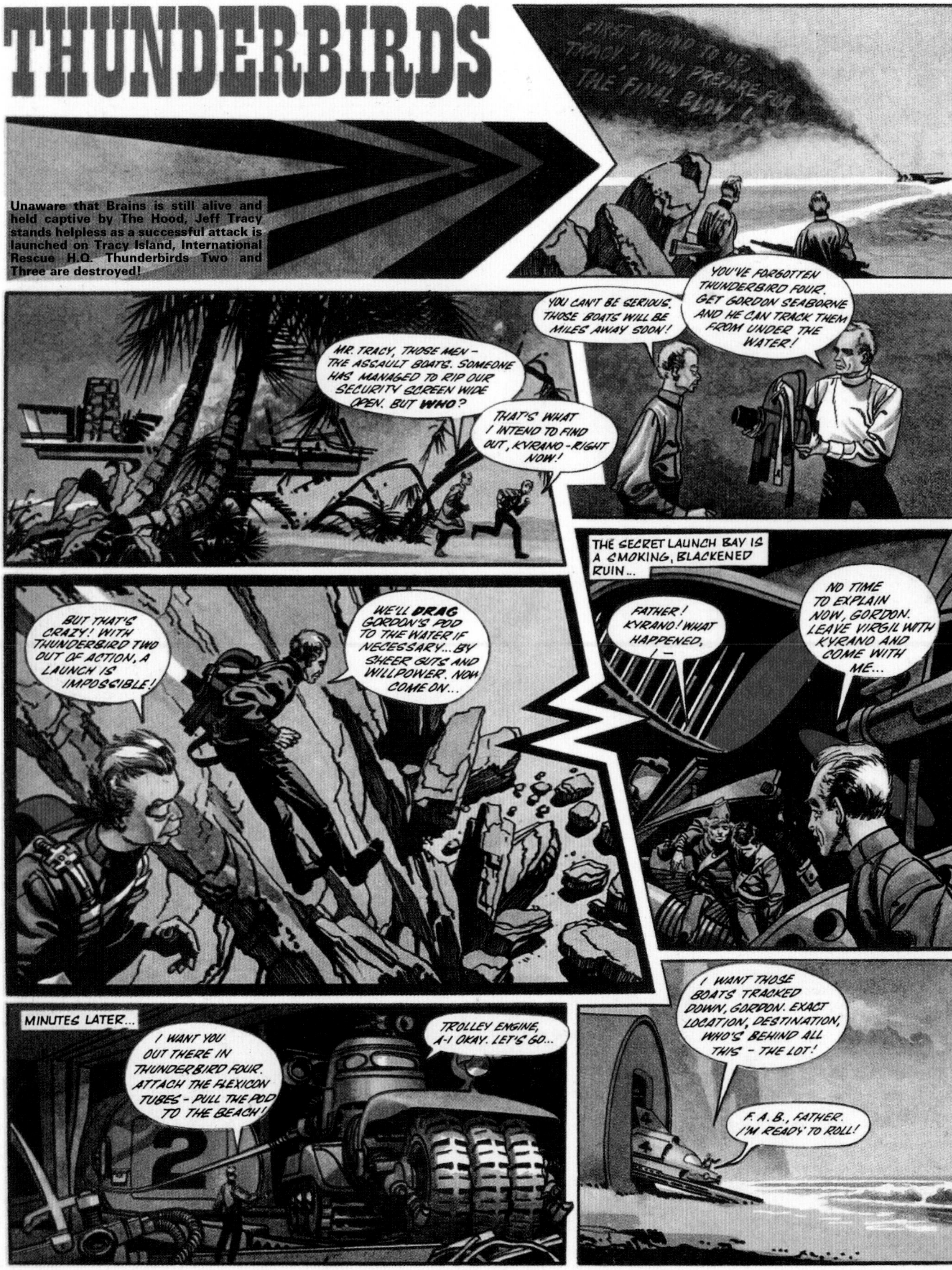
THUNDERBIRDS
FIRST ROUND TO ME, TRACY! NOW PREPARE FOR THE FINAL BLOW!
Unaware that Brains is still alive and held captive by The Hood, Jeff Tracy stands helpless as a successful attack is launched on Tracy Island, International Rescue H.Q. Thunderbirds Two and Three are destroyed!
MR. TRACY, THOSE MEN - THE ASSAULT BOATS. SOMEONE HAS MANAGED TO RIP OUR SECURITY SCREEN WIDE OPEN. BUT WHO?
THAT'S WHAT I INTEND TO FIND OUT, KYRANO - RIGHT NOW!
YOU CAN'T BE SERIOUS. THOSE BOATS WILL BE MILES AWAY SOON!
YOU'VE FORGOTTEN THUNDERBIRD FOUR. GET GORDON SEABORNE AND HE CAN TRACK THEM FROM UNDER THE WATER!
THE SECRET LAUNCH BAY IS A SMOKING, BLACKENED RUIN...
FATHER! KYRANO! WHAT HAPPENED, I -
NO TIME TO EXPLAIN NOW, GORDON. LEAVE VIRGIL WITH KYRANO AND COME WITH ME...
BUT THAT'S CRAZY! WITH THUNDERBIRD TWO OUT OF ACTION, A LAUNCH IS IMPOSSIBLE!
WE'LL DRAG GORDON'S POD TO THE WATER IF NECESSARY... BY SHEER GUTS AND WILLPOWER. NOW COME ON...
MINUTES LATER...
I WANT YOU OUT THERE IN THUNDERBIRD FOUR. ATTACH THE FLEXICON TUBES - PULL THE POD TO THE BEACH!
TROLLEY ENGINE, A-1 OKAY. LET'S GO...
I WANT THOSE BOATS TRACKED DOWN, GORDON. EXACT LOCATION, DESTINATION, WHO'S BEHIND ALL THIS - THE LOT!
F.A.B., FATHER. I'M READY TO ROLL!

Artist: Frank Bellamy

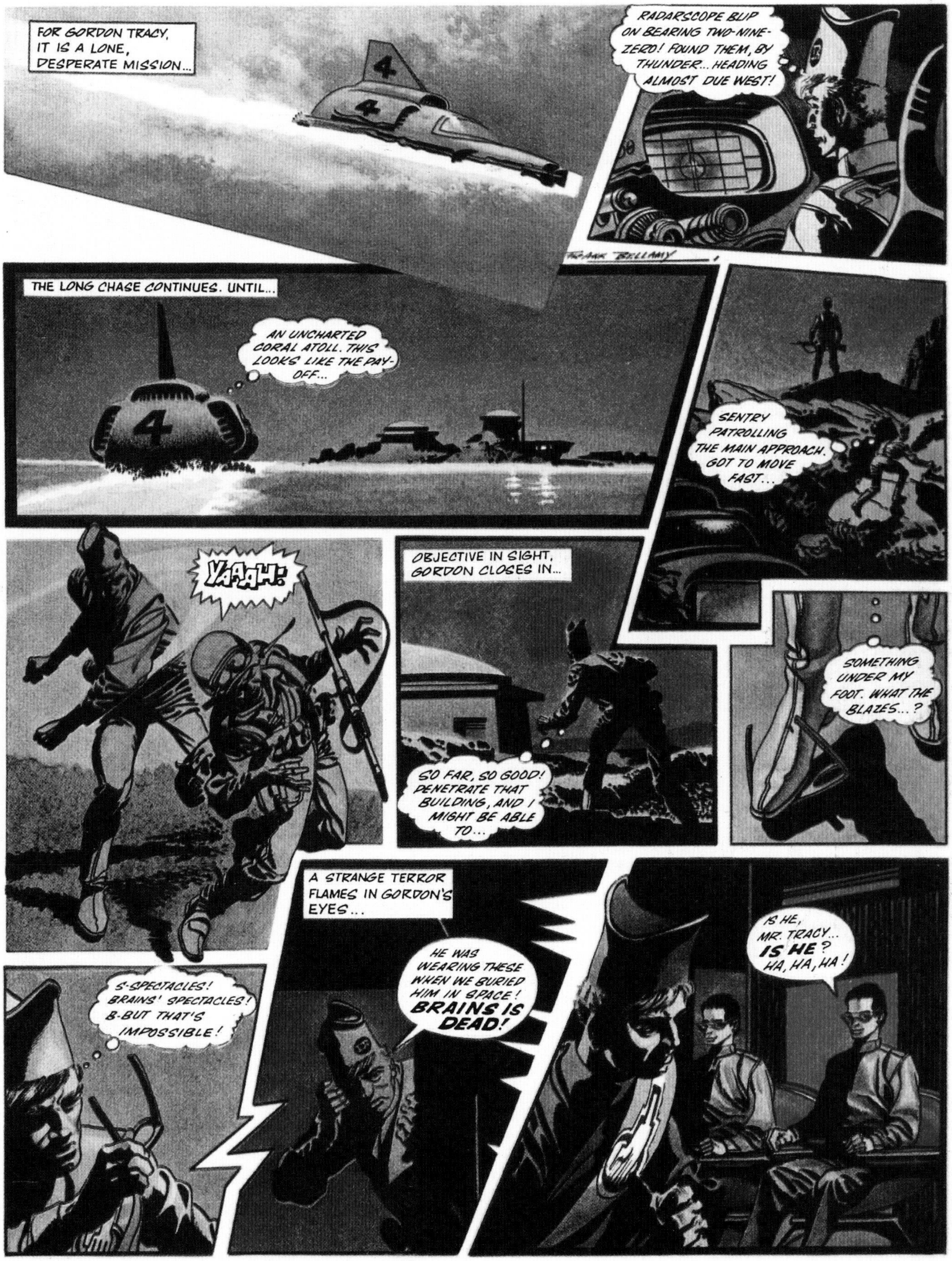
FOR GORDON TRACY, IT IS A LONE, DESPERATE MISSION...
RADARSCOPE BLIP ON BEARING TWO-NINE-ZERO! FOUND THEM, BY THUNDER... HEADING ALMOST DUE WEST!
FRANK BELLAMY
THE LONG CHASE CONTINUES. UNTIL...
AN UNCHARTED CORAL ATOLL. THIS LOOKS LIKE THE PAY-OFF...
SENTRY PATROLLING THE MAIN APPROACH. GOT TO MOVE FAST...
YAAAH!
OBJECTIVE IN SIGHT, GORDON CLOSES IN...
SO FAR, SO GOOD! PENETRATE THAT BUILDING, AND I MIGHT BE ABLE TO...
SOMETHING UNDER MY FOOT. WHAT THE BLAZES...?
S-SPECTACLES! BRAINS' SPECTACLES! B-BUT THAT'S IMPOSSIBLE!
A STRANGE TERROR FLAMES IN GORDON'S EYES...
HE WAS WEARING THESE WHEN WE BURIED HIM IN SPACE! BRAINS IS DEAD!
IS HE, MR. TRACY... IS HE? HA, HA, HA!

Part 6 - dateline 30 March 2068

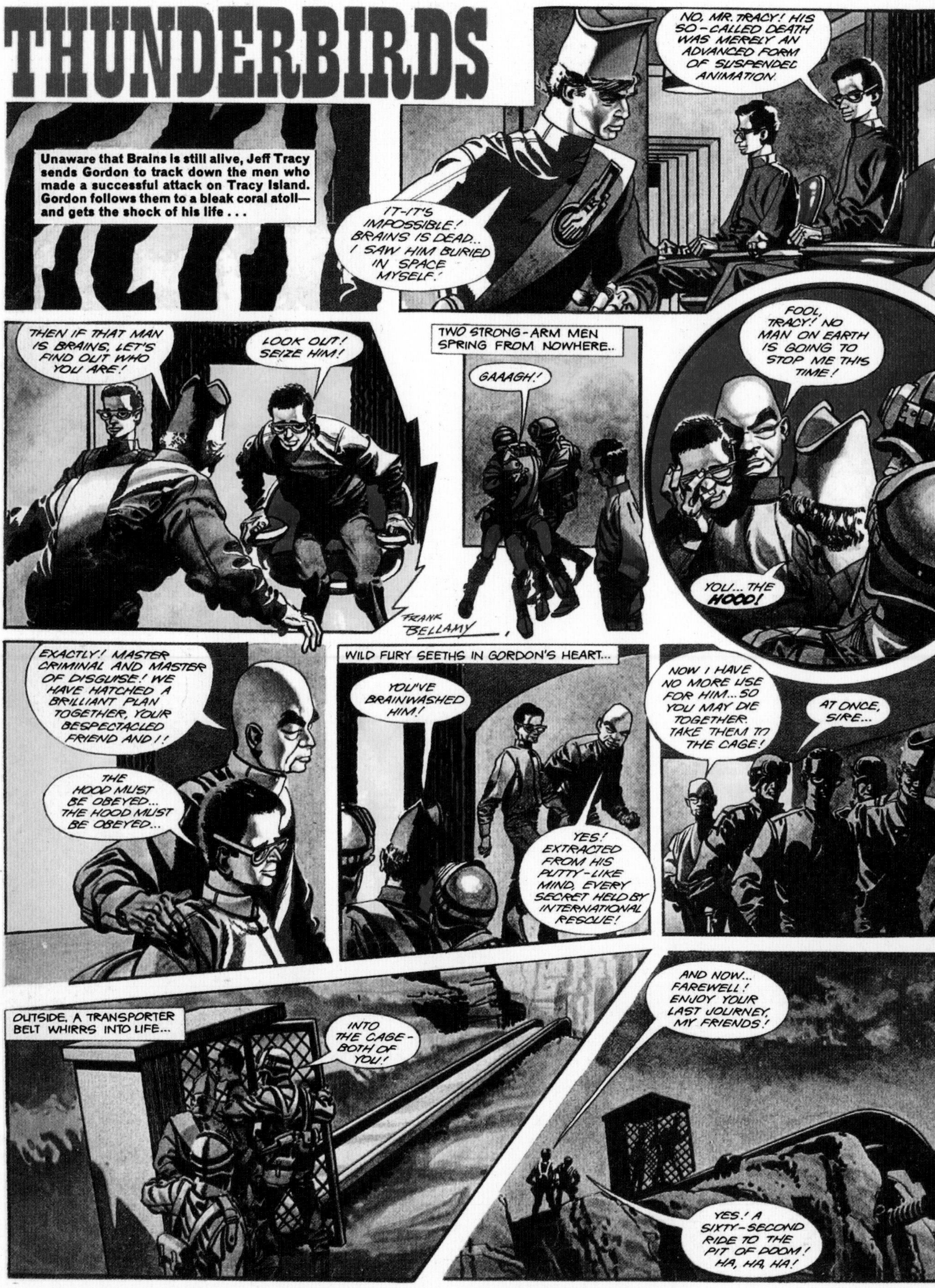
THUNDERBIRDS
Unaware that Brains is still alive, Jeff Tracy sends Gordon to track down the men who made a successful attack on Tracy Island. Gordon follows them to a bleak coral atoll— and gets the shock of his life . . .
IT-IT'S IMPOSSIBLE! BRAINS IS DEAD... I SAW HIM BURIED IN SPACE MYSELF!
NO, MR. TRACY! HIS SO-CALLED DEATH WAS MERELY AN ADVANCED FORM OF SUSPENDED ANIMATION.
THEN IF THAT MAN IS BRAINS, LET'S FIND OUT WHO YOU ARE!
LOOK OUT! SEIZE HIM!
TWO STRONG-ARM MEN SPRING FROM NOWHERE..
GAAAGH!
FRANK BELLAMY
FOOL, TRACY! NO MAN ON EARTH IS GOING TO STOP ME THIS TIME!
YOU... THE HOOD!
EXACTLY! MASTER CRIMINAL AND MASTER OF DISGUISE! WE HAVE HATCHED A BRILLIANT PLAN TOGETHER, YOUR BESPECTACLED FRIEND AND I!
THE HOOD MUST BE OBEYED... THE HOOD MUST BE OBEYED...
WILD FURY SEETHS IN GORDON'S HEART...
YOU'VE BRAINWASHED HIM!
YES! EXTRACTED FROM HIS PUTTY-LIKE MIND, EVERY SECRET HELD BY INTERNATIONAL RESCUE!
NOW I HAVE NO MORE USE FOR HIM... SO YOU MAY DIE TOGETHER. TAKE THEM TO THE CAGE!
AT ONCE, SIRE...
OUTSIDE, A TRANSPORTER BELT WHIRRS INTO LIFE...
INTO THE CAGE- BOTH OF YOU!
AND NOW... FAREWELL! ENJOY YOUR LAST JOURNEY, MY FRIENDS!
YES! A SIXTY-SECOND RIDE TO THE PIT OF DOOM! HA, HA, HA!

Artist: Frank Bellamy

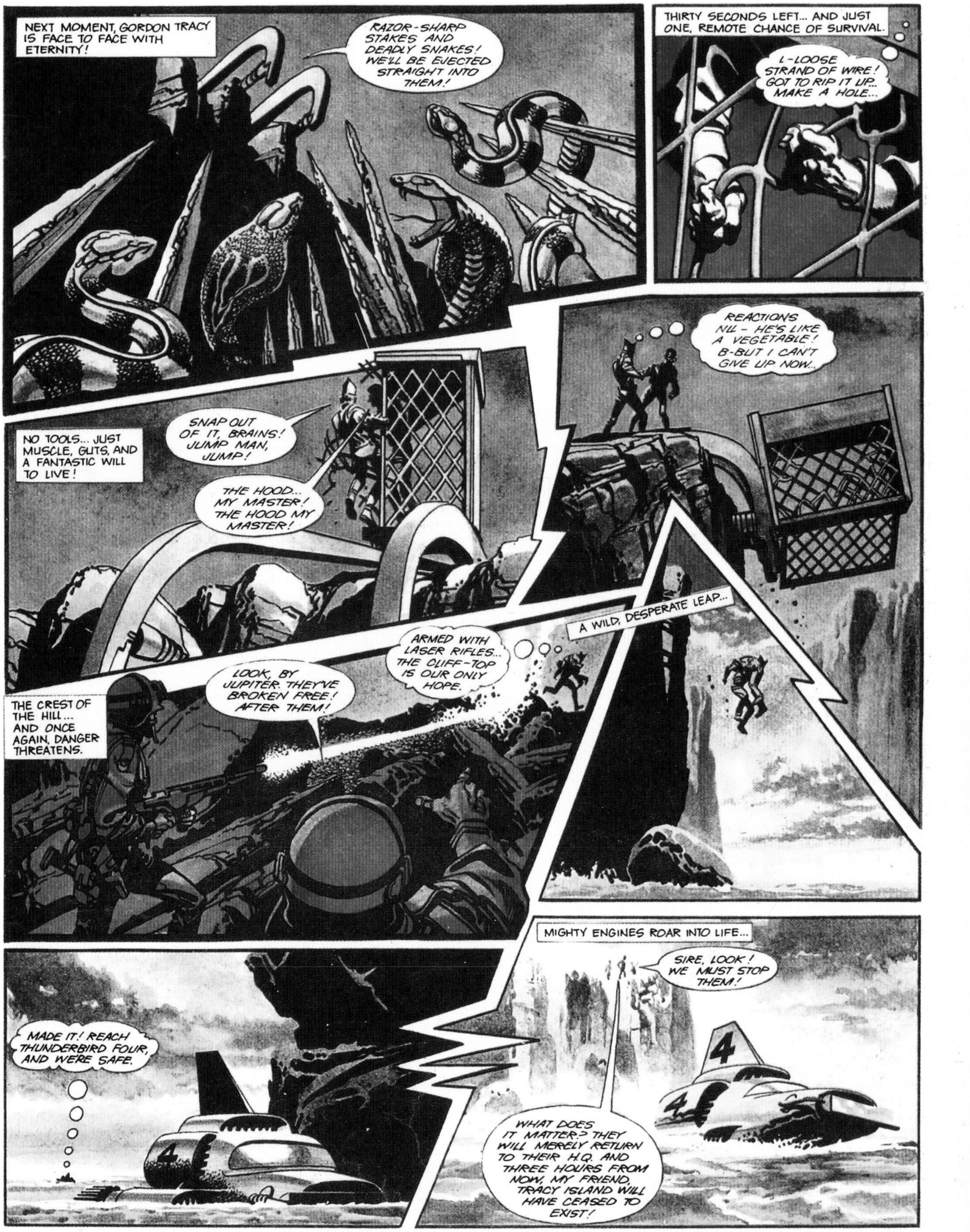
NEXT MOMENT, GORDON TRACY IS FACE TO FACE WITH ETERNITY!
RAZOR-SHARP STAKES AND DEADLY SNAKES! WE'LL BE EJECTED STRAIGHT INTO THEM!
THIRTY SECONDS LEFT... AND JUST ONE, REMOTE CHANCE OF SURVIVAL.
L-LOOSE STRAND OF WIRE! GOT TO RIP IT UP... MAKE A HOLE...
NO TOOLS... JUST MUSCLE, GUTS, AND A FANTASTIC WILL TO LIVE!
SNAP OUT OF IT, BRAINS! JUMP MAN, JUMP!
THE HOOD... MY MASTER! THE HOOD MY MASTER!
REACTIONS NIL - HE'S LIKE A VEGETABLE! B-BUT I CAN'T GIVE UP NOW...
A WILD, DESPERATE LEAP...
THE CREST OF THE HILL... AND ONCE AGAIN, DANGER THREATENS.
LOOK, BY JUPITER. THEY'VE BROKEN FREE! AFTER THEM!
ARMED WITH LASER RIFLES... THE CLIFF-TOP IS OUR ONLY HOPE.
MADE IT! REACH THUNDERBIRD FOUR, AND WE'RE SAFE.
MIGHTY ENGINES ROAR INTO LIFE...
SIRE, LOOK! WE MUST STOP THEM!
WHAT DOES IT MATTER? THEY WILL MERELY RETURN TO THEIR H.Q. AND THREE HOURS FROM NOW, MY FRIEND, TRACY ISLAND WILL HAVE CEASED TO EXIST!

Part 7 - dateline 06 April 2068

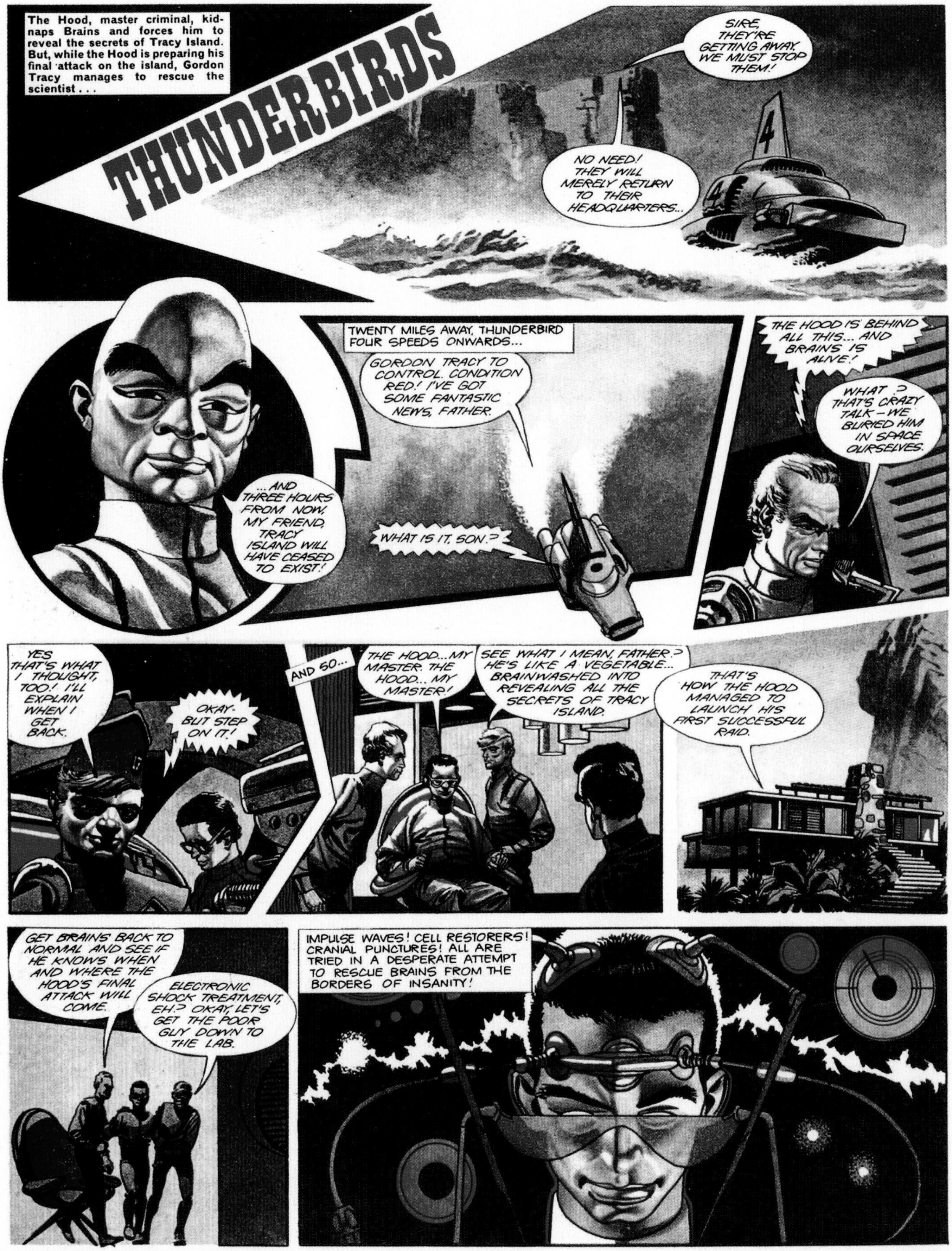
The Hood, master criminal, kidnaps Brains and forces him to reveal the secrets of Tracy Island. But, while the Hood is preparing his final attack on the island, Gordon Tracy manages to rescue the scientist . . .
THUNDERBIRDS
SIRE, THEY'RE GETTING AWAY. WE MUST STOP THEM!
NO NEED! THEY WILL MERELY RETURN TO THEIR HEADQUARTERS...
...AND THREE HOURS FROM NOW, MY FRIEND, TRACY ISLAND WILL HAVE CEASED TO EXIST!
TWENTY MILES AWAY, THUNDERBIRD FOUR SPEEDS ONWARDS...
GORDON TRACY TO CONTROL. CONDITION RED! I'VE GOT SOME FANTASTIC NEWS, FATHER.
WHAT IS IT, SON.?
THE HOOD IS BEHIND ALL THIS... AND BRAINS IS ALIVE!
WHAT ? THAT'S CRAZY TALK—WE BURIED HIM IN SPACE OURSELVES.
YES THAT'S WHAT I THOUGHT, TOO! I'LL EXPLAIN WHEN I GET BACK.
OKAY- BUT STEP ON IT!
AND SO...
THE HOOD...MY MASTER. THE HOOD... MY MASTER!
SEE WHAT I MEAN, FATHER.? HE'S LIKE A VEGETABLE... BRAINWASHED INTO REVEALING ALL THE SECRETS OF TRACY ISLAND.
THAT'S HOW THE HOOD MANAGED TO LAUNCH HIS FIRST SUCCESSFUL RAID.
GET BRAINS BACK TO NORMAL AND SEE IF HE KNOWS WHEN AND WHERE THE HOOD'S FINAL ATTACK WILL COME.
ELECTRONIC SHOCK TREATMENT, EH.? OKAY, LET'S GET THE POOR GUY DOWN TO THE LAB.
IMPULSE WAVES! CELL RESTORERS! CRANIAL PUNCTURES! ALL ARE TRIED IN A DESPERATE ATTEMPT TO RESCUE BRAINS FROM THE BORDERS OF INSANITY!

Artist: Frank Bellamy

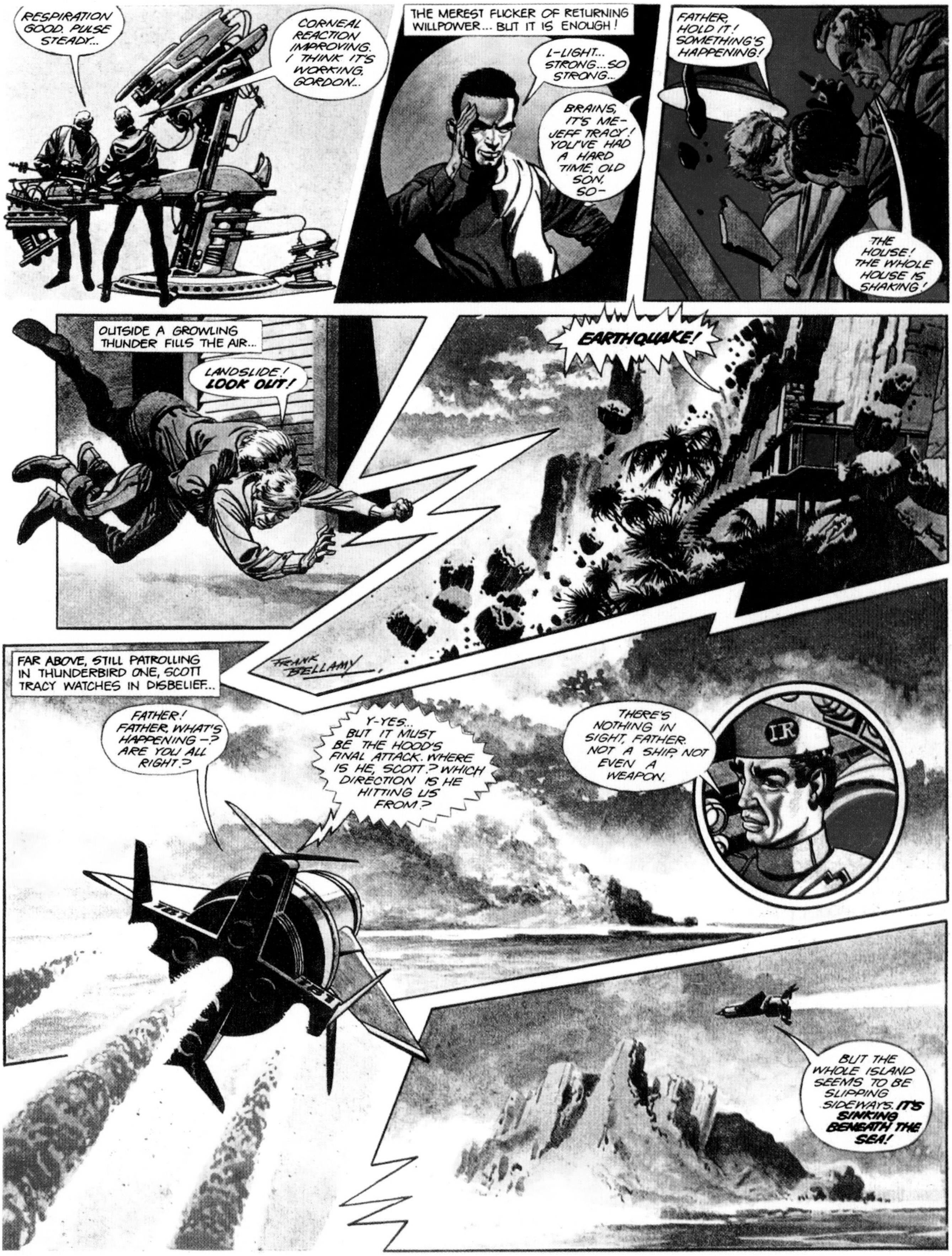
RESPIRATION GOOD. PULSE STEADY...
CORNEAL REACTION IMPROVING. I THINK IT'S WORKING, GORDON..
THE MEREST FLICKER OF RETURNING WILLPOWER... BUT IT IS ENOUGH!
L-LIGHT... STRONG... SO STRONG...
BRAINS, IT'S ME- JEFF TRACY! YOU'VE HAD A HARD TIME, OLD SON, SO-
FATHER, HOLD IT! SOMETHING'S HAPPENING!
THE HOUSE! THE WHOLE HOUSE IS SHAKING!
OUTSIDE A GROWLING THUNDER FILLS THE AIR...
LANDSLIDE! LOOK OUT!
EARTHQUAKE!
FRANK BELLAMY
FAR ABOVE, STILL PATROLLING IN THUNDERBIRD ONE, SCOTT TRACY WATCHES IN DISBELIEF...
FATHER! FATHER, WHAT'S HAPPENING -? ARE YOU ALL RIGHT?
Y-YES... BUT IT MUST BE THE HOOD'S FINAL ATTACK. WHERE IS HE, SCOTT? WHICH DIRECTION IS HE HITTING US FROM?
THERE'S NOTHING IN SIGHT, FATHER. NOT A SHIP, NOT EVEN A WEAPON.
BUT THE WHOLE ISLAND SEEMS TO BE SLIPPING SIDEWAYS. IT'S SINKING BENEATH THE SEA!

Part 8 - dateline 13 April 2068

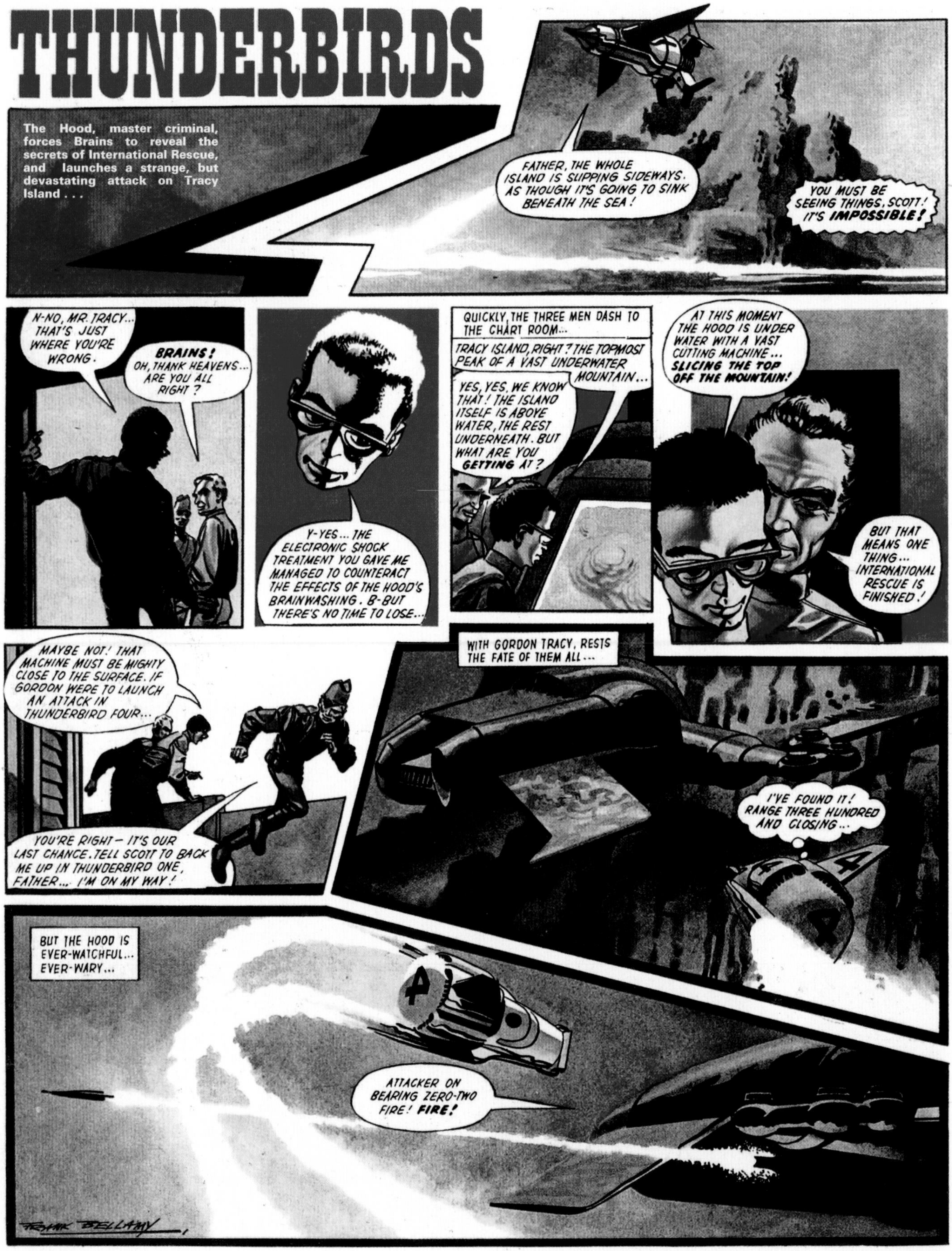
THUNDERBIRDS
The Hood, master criminal, forces Brains to reveal the secrets of International Rescue, and launches a strange, but devastating attack on Tracy Island . . .
FATHER, THE WHOLE ISLAND IS SLIPPING SIDEWAYS. AS THOUGH IT'S GOING TO SINK BENEATH THE SEA!
YOU MUST BE SEEING THINGS, SCOTT! IT'S IMPOSSIBLE!
N-NO, MR. TRACY... THAT'S JUST WHERE YOU'RE WRONG.
BRAINS! OH, THANK HEAVENS... ARE YOU ALL RIGHT?
Y-YES... THE ELECTRONIC SHOCK TREATMENT YOU GAVE ME MANAGED TO COUNTERACT THE EFFECTS OF THE HOOD'S BRAINWASHING. B-BUT THERE'S NO TIME TO LOSE...
QUICKLY, THE THREE MEN DASH TO THE CHART ROOM...
TRACY ISLAND, RIGHT? THE TOPMOST PEAK OF A VAST UNDERWATER MOUNTAIN...
YES, YES, WE KNOW THAT! THE ISLAND ITSELF IS ABOVE WATER, THE REST UNDERNEATH. BUT WHAT ARE YOU GETTING AT?
AT THIS MOMENT THE HOOD IS UNDER WATER WITH A VAST CUTTING MACHINE... SLICING THE TOP OFF THE MOUNTAIN!
BUT THAT MEANS ONE THING... INTERNATIONAL RESCUE IS FINISHED!
MAYBE NOT! THAT MACHINE MUST BE MIGHTY CLOSE TO THE SURFACE. IF GORDON WERE TO LAUNCH AN ATTACK IN THUNDERBIRD FOUR...
YOU'RE RIGHT – IT'S OUR LAST CHANCE. TELL SCOTT TO BACK ME UP IN THUNDERBIRD ONE, FATHER... I'M ON MY WAY!
WITH GORDON TRACY, RESTS THE FATE OF THEM ALL...
I'VE FOUND IT! RANGE THREE HUNDRED AND CLOSING...
BUT THE HOOD IS EVER-WATCHFUL... EVER-WARY...
ATTACKER ON BEARING ZERO-TWO FIRE! FIRE!
FRANK BELLAMY

Artist: Frank Bellamy

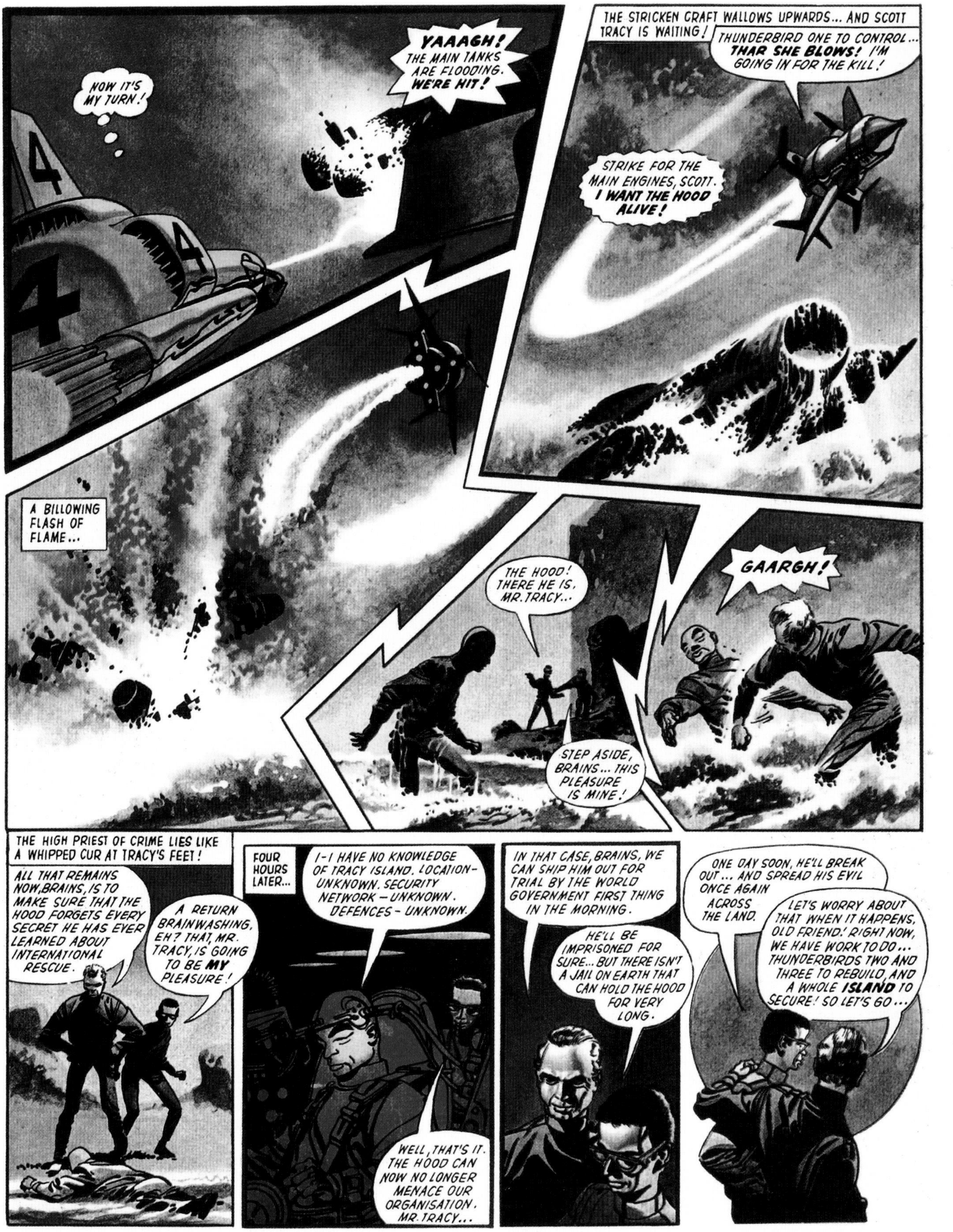
NOW IT'S MY TURN!
YAAAGH! THE MAIN TANKS ARE FLOODING. WE'RE HIT!
THE STRICKEN CRAFT WALLOWS UPWARDS... AND SCOTT TRACY IS WAITING!
THUNDERBIRD ONE TO CONTROL... THAR SHE BLOWS! I'M GOING IN FOR THE KILL!
STRIKE FOR THE MAIN ENGINES, SCOTT. I WANT THE HOOD ALIVE!
A BILLOWING FLASH OF FLAME...
THE HOOD! THERE HE IS, MR. TRACY...
STEP ASIDE, BRAINS... THIS PLEASURE IS MINE!
GAARGH!
THE HIGH PRIEST OF CRIME LIES LIKE A WHIPPED CUR AT TRACY'S FEET!
ALL THAT REMAINS NOW, BRAINS, IS TO MAKE SURE THAT THE HOOD FORGETS EVERY SECRET HE HAS EVER LEARNED ABOUT INTERNATIONAL RESCUE.
A RETURN BRAINWASHING, EH? THAT, MR. TRACY, IS GOING TO BE MY PLEASURE!
FOUR HOURS LATER...
I-I HAVE NO KNOWLEDGE OF TRACY ISLAND. LOCATION-UNKNOWN. SECURITY NETWORK — UNKNOWN. DEFENCES - UNKNOWN.
WELL, THAT'S IT. THE HOOD CAN NOW NO LONGER MENACE OUR ORGANISATION, MR. TRACY...
IN THAT CASE, BRAINS, WE CAN SHIP HIM OUT FOR TRIAL BY THE WORLD GOVERNMENT FIRST THING IN THE MORNING.
HE'LL BE IMPRISONED FOR SURE... BUT THERE ISN'T A JAIL ON EARTH THAT CAN HOLD THE HOOD FOR VERY LONG.
ONE DAY SOON, HE'LL BREAK OUT... AND SPREAD HIS EVIL ONCE AGAIN ACROSS THE LAND.
LET'S WORRY ABOUT THAT WHEN IT HAPPENS, OLD FRIEND! RIGHT NOW, WE HAVE WORK TO DO... THUNDERBIRDS TWO AND THREE TO REBUILD, AND A WHOLE ISLAND TO SECURE! SO LET'S GO...

Part 1 - dateline 20 April 2068

Artist: Frank Bellamy

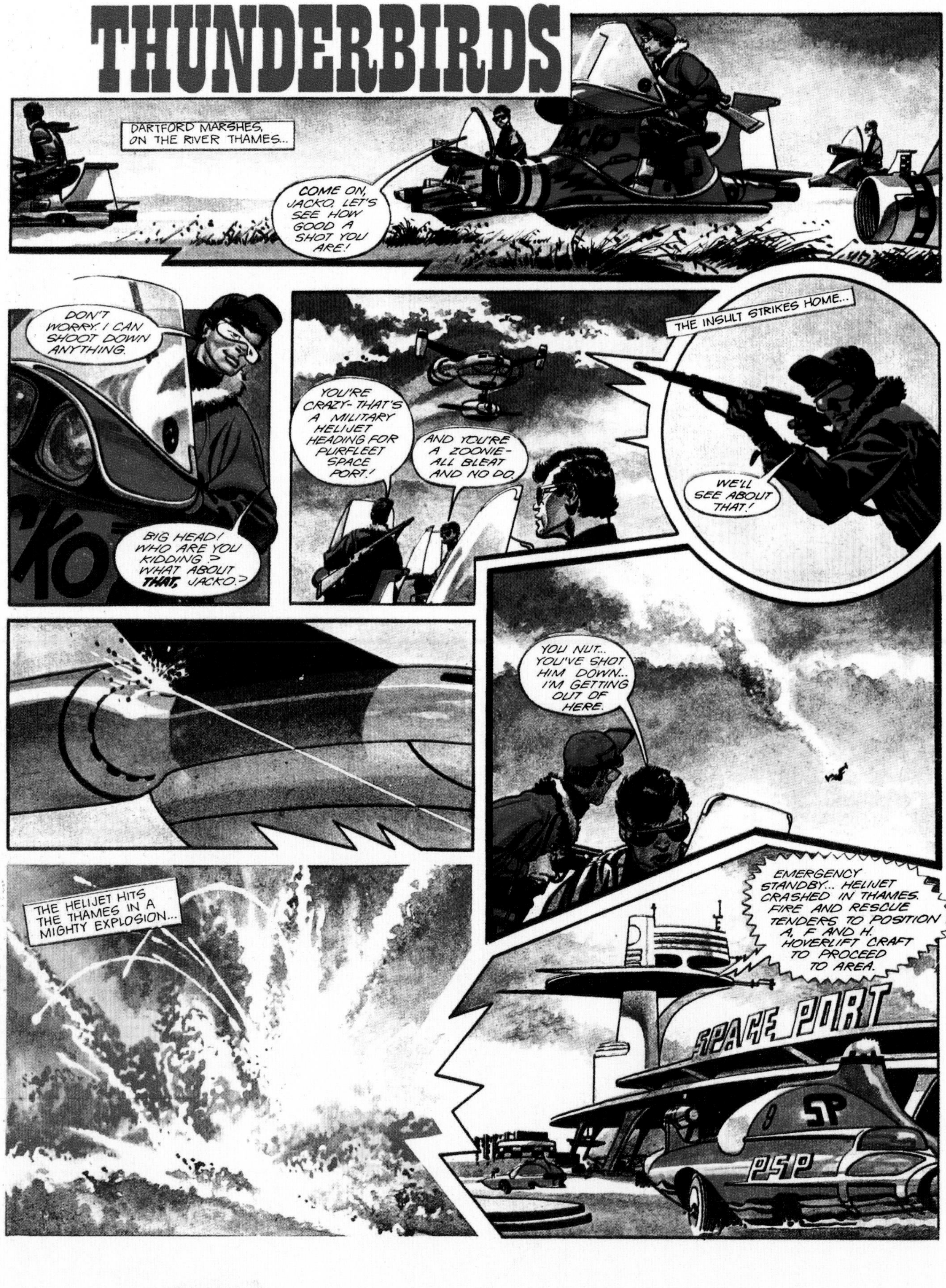
THUNDERBIRDS
DARTFORD MARSHES, ON THE RIVER THAMES...
COME ON, JACKO, LET'S SEE HOW GOOD A SHOT YOU ARE!
DON'T WORRY. I CAN SHOOT DOWN ANYTHING.
BIG HEAD! WHO ARE YOU KIDDING? WHAT ABOUT THAT, JACKO?
YOU'RE CRAZY- THAT'S A MILITARY HELIJET HEADING FOR PURFLEET SPACE PORT!
AND YOU'RE A ZOONIE- ALL BLEAT AND NO DO.
THE INSULT STRIKES HOME...
WE'LL SEE ABOUT THAT!
YOU NUT... YOU'VE SHOT HIM DOWN... I'M GETTING OUT OF HERE.
THE HELIJET HITS THE THAMES IN A MIGHTY EXPLOSION...
EMERGENCY STANDBY... HELIJET CRASHED IN THAMES. FIRE AND RESCUE TENDERS TO POSITION A, F AND H. HOVERLIFT CRAFT TO PROCEED TO AREA.
SPACE PORT
SP
PSP

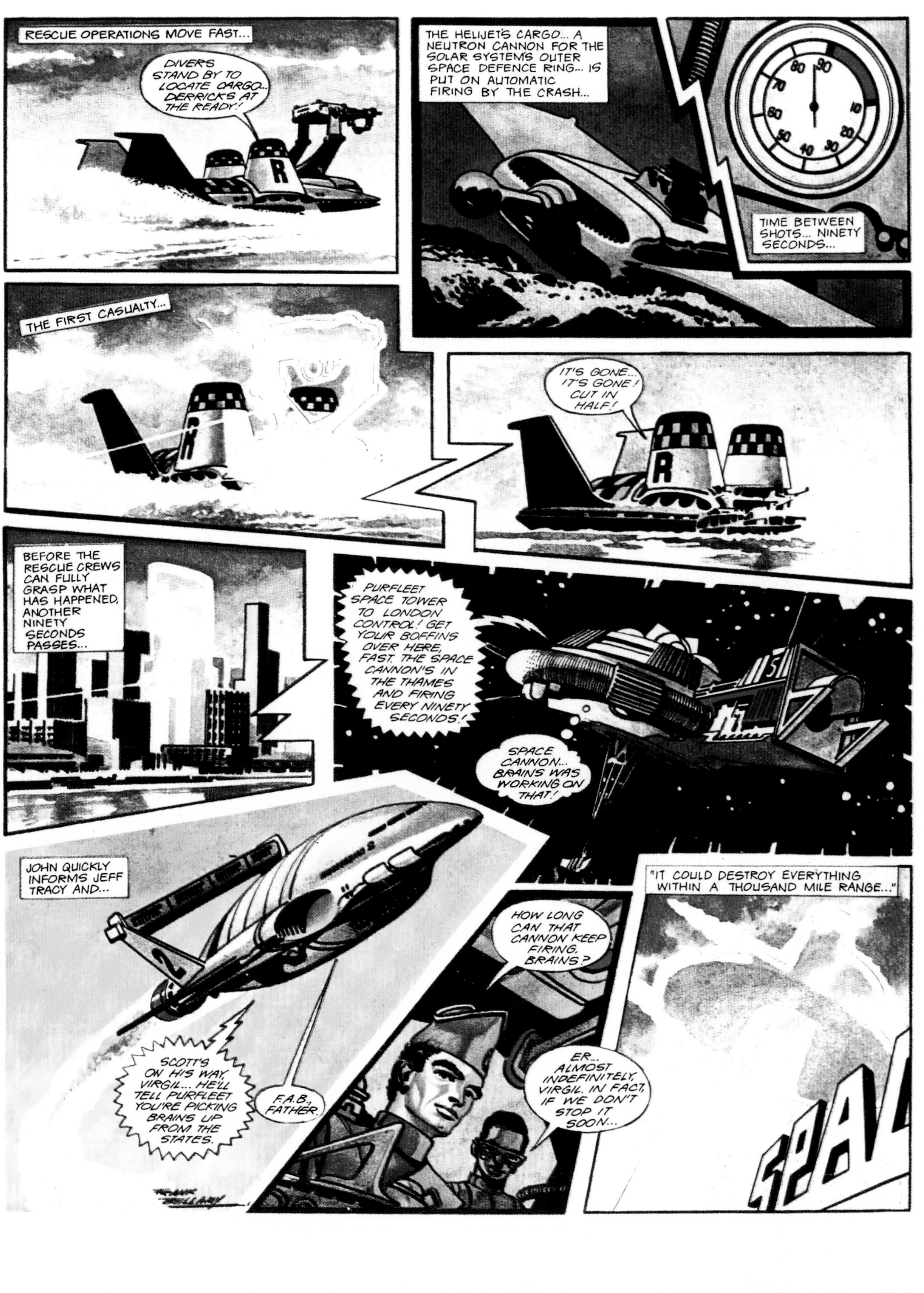
RESCUE OPERATIONS MOVE FAST...
DIVERS STAND BY TO LOCATE CARGO... DERRICKS AT THE READY!
THE HELIJET'S CARGO... A NEUTRON CANNON FOR THE SOLAR SYSTEM'S OUTER SPACE DEFENCE RING... IS PUT ON AUTOMATIC FIRING BY THE CRASH...
TIME BETWEEN SHOTS... NINETY SECONDS...
THE FIRST CASUALTY...
IT'S GONE... IT'S GONE! CUT IN HALF!
BEFORE THE RESCUE CREWS CAN FULLY GRASP WHAT HAS HAPPENED, ANOTHER NINETY SECONDS PASSES...
PURFLEET SPACE TOWER TO LONDON CONTROL! GET YOUR BOFFINS OVER HERE, FAST. THE SPACE CANNON'S IN THE THAMES AND FIRING EVERY NINETY SECONDS!
SPACE CANNON... BRAINS WAS WORKING ON THAT!
JOHN QUICKLY INFORMS JEFF TRACY AND...
SCOTT'S ON HIS WAY, VIRGIL... HE'LL TELL PURFLEET YOU'RE PICKING BRAINS UP FROM THE STATES.
F.A.B., FATHER.
HOW LONG CAN THAT CANNON KEEP FIRING, BRAINS?
ER... ALMOST INDEFINITELY, VIRGIL. IN FACT, IF WE DON'T STOP IT SOON...
"IT COULD DESTROY EVERYTHING WITHIN A THOUSAND MILE RANGE..."

Part 2 - dateline 27 April 2068

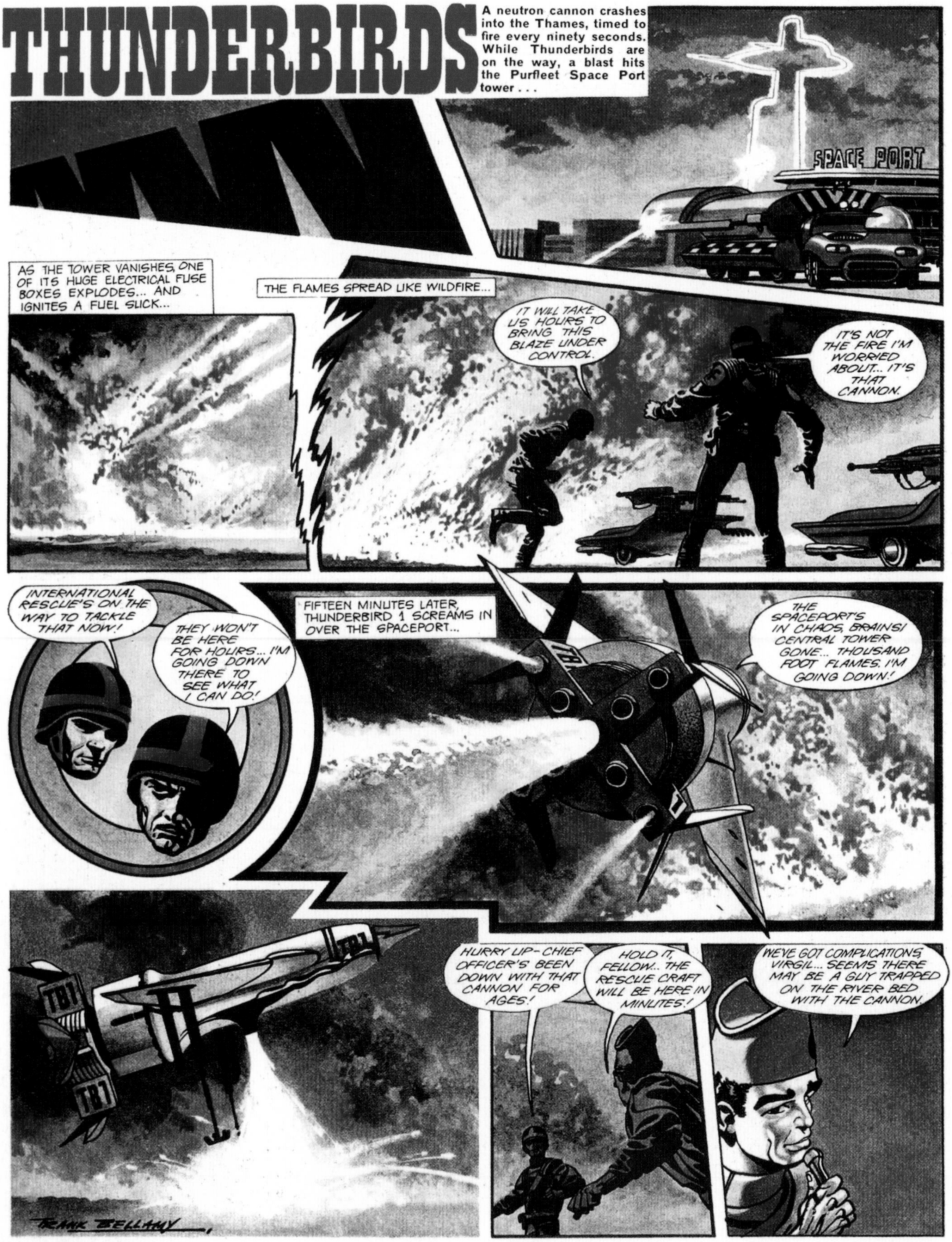
THUNDERBIRDS
A neutron cannon crashes into the Thames, timed to fire every ninety seconds. While Thunderbirds are on the way, a blast hits the Purfleet Space Port tower . . .
SPACE PORT
AS THE TOWER VANISHES, ONE OF ITS HUGE ELECTRICAL FUSE BOXES EXPLODES... AND IGNITES A FUEL SLICK...
THE FLAMES SPREAD LIKE WILDFIRE...
IT WILL TAKE US HOURS TO BRING THIS BLAZE UNDER CONTROL.
IT'S NOT THE FIRE I'M WORRIED ABOUT... IT'S THAT CANNON.
INTERNATIONAL RESCUE'S ON THE WAY TO TACKLE THAT NOW!
THEY WON'T BE HERE FOR HOURS... I'M GOING DOWN THERE TO SEE WHAT I CAN DO!
FIFTEEN MINUTES LATER, THUNDERBIRD 1 SCREAMS IN OVER THE SPACEPORT...
THE SPACEPORT'S IN CHAOS, BRAINS! CENTRAL TOWER GONE... THOUSAND FOOT FLAMES. I'M GOING DOWN!
HURRY UP- CHIEF OFFICER'S BEEN DOWN WITH THAT CANNON FOR AGES!
HOLD IT, FELLOW... THE RESCUE CRAFT WILL BE HERE IN MINUTES!
WE'VE GOT COMPLICATIONS, VIRGIL... SEEMS THERE MAY BE A GUY TRAPPED ON THE RIVER BED WITH THE CANNON.
FRANK BELLAMY

Artist: Frank Bellamy

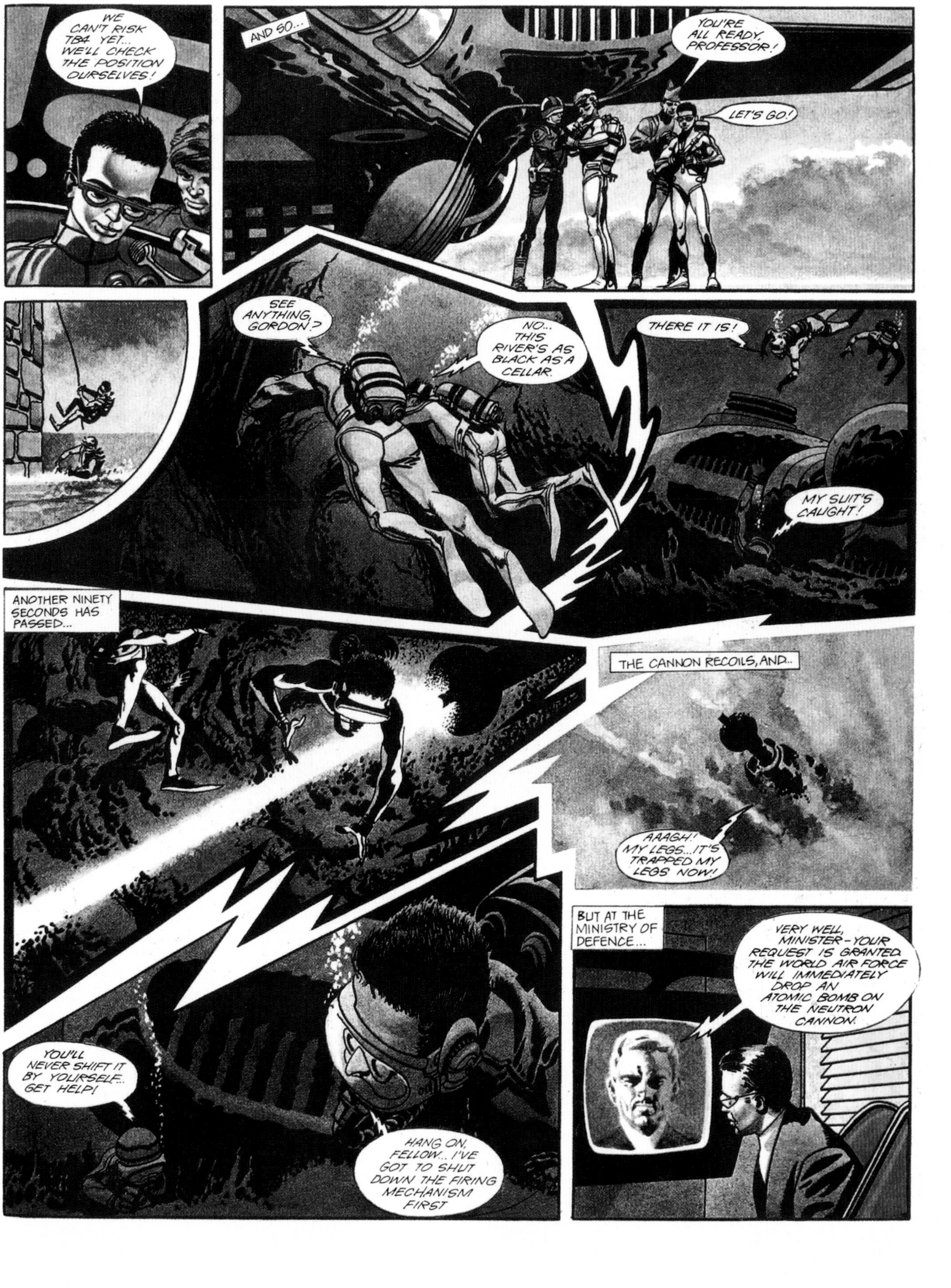
WE CAN'T RISK TB4 YET... WE'LL CHECK THE POSITION OURSELVES!
AND SO...
YOU'RE ALL READY, PROFESSOR!
LET'S GO!
SEE ANYTHING, GORDON?
NO... THIS RIVER'S AS BLACK AS A CELLAR.
THERE IT IS!
MY SUIT'S CAUGHT!
ANOTHER NINETY SECONDS HAS PASSED...
THE CANNON RECOILS, AND..
AAAGH! MY LEGS...IT'S TRAPPED MY LEGS NOW!
YOU'LL NEVER SHIFT IT BY YOURSELF... GET HELP!
HANG ON, FELLOW... I'VE GOT TO SHUT DOWN THE FIRING MECHANISM FIRST
BUT AT THE MINISTRY OF DEFENCE...
VERY WELL, MINISTER - YOUR REQUEST IS GRANTED. THE WORLD AIR FORCE WILL IMMEDIATELY DROP AN ATOMIC BOMB ON THE NEUTRON CANNON.

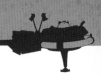

Part 3 - dateline 04 May 2068

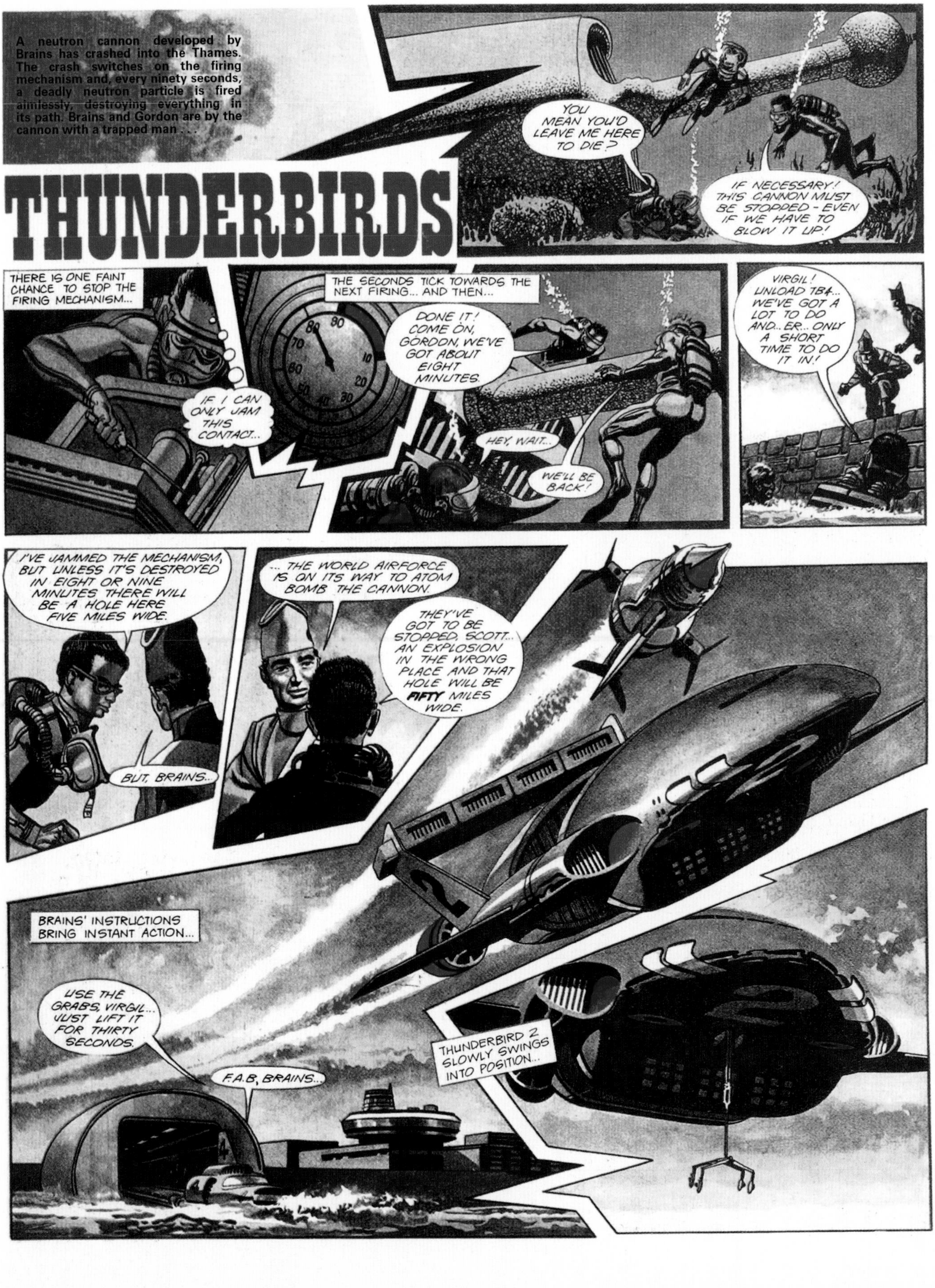
A neutron cannon developed by Brains has crashed into the Thames. The crash switches on the firing mechanism and, every ninety seconds, a deadly neutron particle is fired aimlessly, destroying everything in its path. Brains and Gordon are by the cannon with a trapped man . . .
THUNDERBIRDS
YOU MEAN YOU'D LEAVE ME HERE TO DIE?
IF NECESSARY! THIS CANNON MUST BE STOPPED - EVEN IF WE HAVE TO BLOW IT UP!
THERE IS ONE FAINT CHANCE TO STOP THE FIRING MECHANISM...
IF I CAN ONLY JAM THIS CONTACT...
THE SECONDS TICK TOWARDS THE NEXT FIRING... AND THEN...
DONE IT! COME ON, GORDON, WE'VE GOT ABOUT EIGHT MINUTES.
HEY, WAIT...
WE'LL BE BACK!
VIRGIL! UNLOAD TB4... WE'VE GOT A LOT TO DO AND... ER... ONLY A SHORT TIME TO DO IT IN!
I'VE JAMMED THE MECHANISM, BUT UNLESS IT'S DESTROYED IN EIGHT OR NINE MINUTES THERE WILL BE A HOLE HERE FIVE MILES WIDE.
BUT, BRAINS...
... THE WORLD AIRFORCE IS ON ITS WAY TO ATOM BOMB THE CANNON.
THEY'VE GOT TO BE STOPPED, SCOTT... AN EXPLOSION IN THE WRONG PLACE AND THAT HOLE WILL BE FIFTY MILES WIDE.
BRAINS' INSTRUCTIONS BRING INSTANT ACTION...
USE THE GRABS, VIRGIL... JUST LIFT IT FOR THIRTY SECONDS.
F.A.B. BRAINS...
THUNDERBIRD 2 SLOWLY SWINGS INTO POSITION...

Artist: Frank Bellamy

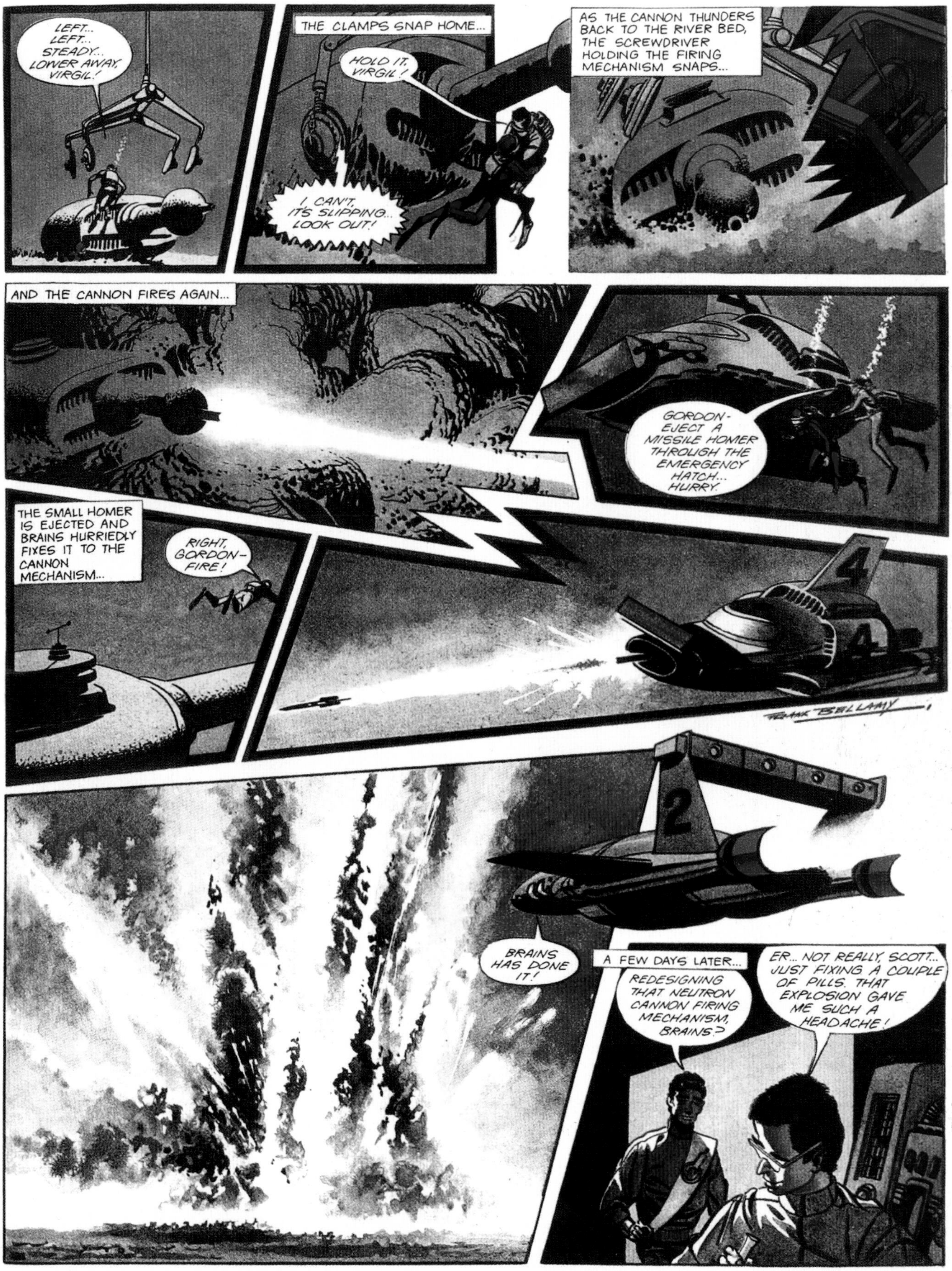
LEFT... LEFT... STEADY... LOWER AWAY, VIRGIL!
THE CLAMPS SNAP HOME...
HOLD IT, VIRGIL!
I CAN'T, IT'S SLIPPING... LOOK OUT!
AS THE CANNON THUNDERS BACK TO THE RIVER BED, THE SCREWDRIVER HOLDING THE FIRING MECHANISM SNAPS...
AND THE CANNON FIRES AGAIN...
GORDON- EJECT A MISSILE HOMER THROUGH THE EMERGENCY HATCH... HURRY.
THE SMALL HOMER IS EJECTED AND BRAINS HURRIEDLY FIXES IT TO THE CANNON MECHANISM...
RIGHT, GORDON- FIRE!
4
4
FRANK BELLAMY
2
BRAINS HAS DONE IT!
A FEW DAYS LATER...
REDESIGNING THAT NEUTRON CANNON FIRING MECHANISM, BRAINS?
ER... NOT REALLY, SCOTT... JUST FIXING A COUPLE OF PILLS. THAT EXPLOSION GAVE ME SUCH A HEADACHE!

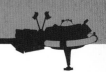

Part 1 - dateline 11 May 2068

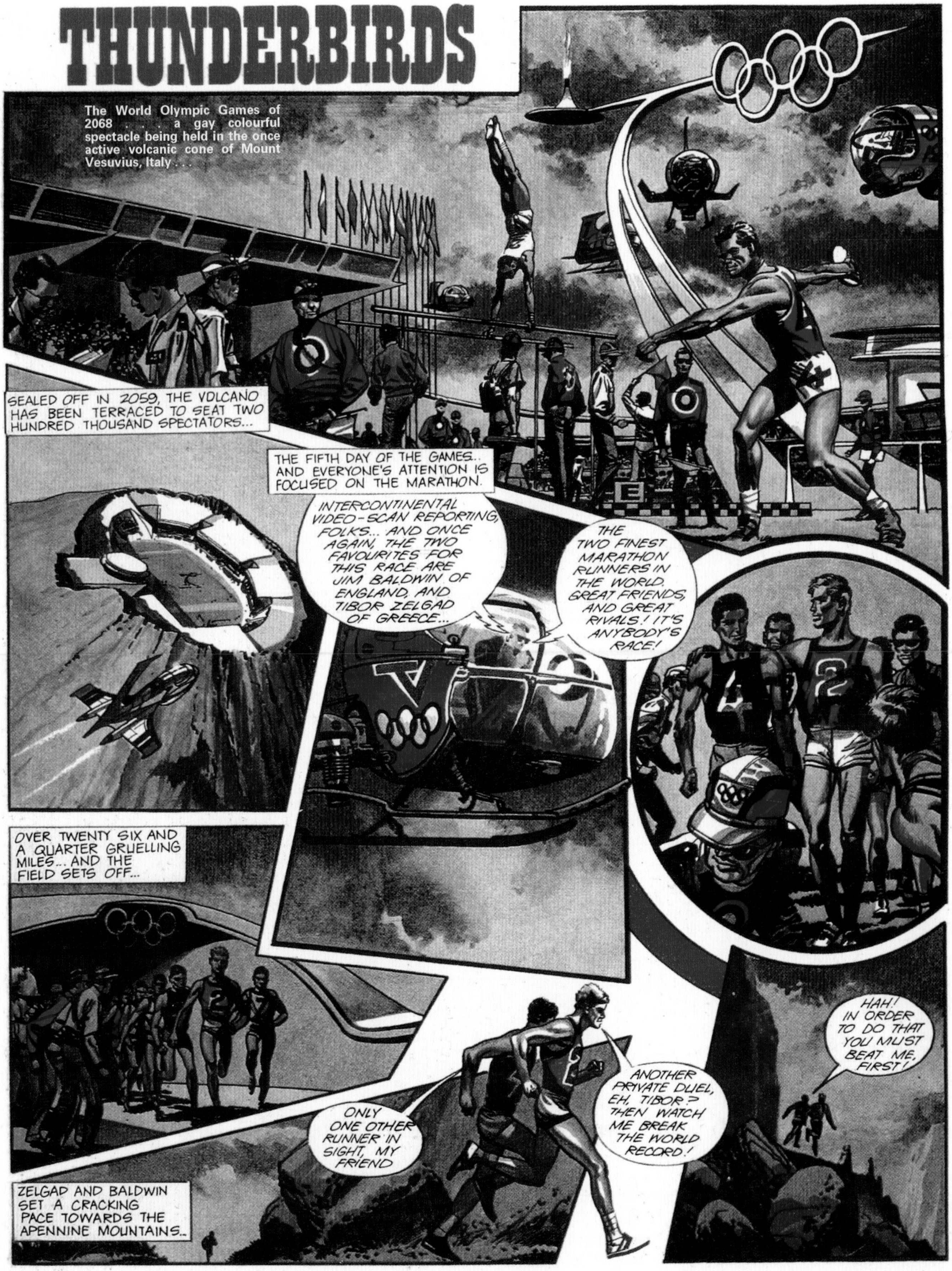
THUNDERBIRDS
The World Olympic Games of 2068 . . . a gay colourful spectacle being held in the once active volcanic cone of Mount Vesuvius, Italy . . .
SEALED OFF IN 2059, THE VOLCANO HAS BEEN TERRACED TO SEAT TWO HUNDRED THOUSAND SPECTATORS...
THE FIFTH DAY OF THE GAMES.. AND EVERYONE'S ATTENTION IS FOCUSED ON THE MARATHON.
INTERCONTINENTAL VIDEO-SCAN REPORTING, FOLKS... AND ONCE AGAIN, THE TWO FAVOURITES FOR THIS RACE ARE JIM BALDWIN OF ENGLAND, AND TIBOR ZELGAD OF GREECE...
THE TWO FINEST MARATHON RUNNERS IN THE WORLD. GREAT FRIENDS, AND GREAT RIVALS! IT'S ANYBODY'S RACE!
OVER TWENTY SIX AND A QUARTER GRUELLING MILES... AND THE FIELD SETS OFF...
ZELGAD AND BALDWIN SET A CRACKING PACE TOWARDS THE APENNINE MOUNTAINS...
ONLY ONE OTHER RUNNER IN SIGHT, MY FRIEND
ANOTHER PRIVATE DUEL, EH, TIBOR? THEN WATCH ME BREAK THE WORLD RECORD!
HAH! IN ORDER TO DO THAT YOU MUST BEAT ME, FIRST!

Artist: Frank Bellamy

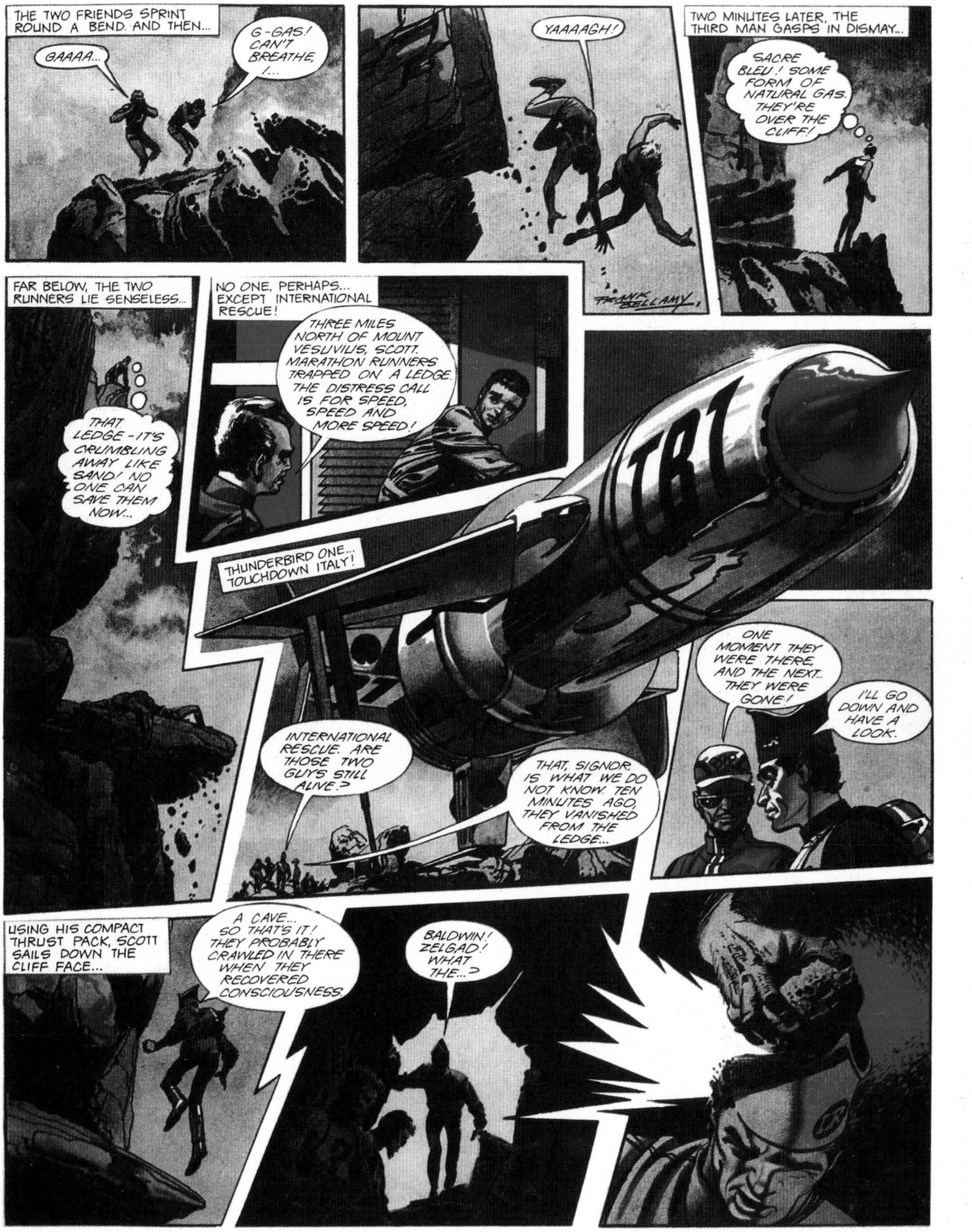
THE TWO FRIENDS SPRINT ROUND A BEND. AND THEN...
GAAAA...
G-GAS! CAN'T BREATHE, I...
YAAAAGH!
TWO MINUTES LATER, THE THIRD MAN GASPS IN DISMAY...
SACRE BLEU! SOME FORM OF NATURAL GAS. THEY'RE OVER THE CLIFF!
FRANK BELLAMY
FAR BELOW, THE TWO RUNNERS LIE SENSELESS...
THAT LEDGE - IT'S CRUMBLING AWAY LIKE SAND! NO ONE CAN SAVE THEM NOW...
NO ONE, PERHAPS... EXCEPT INTERNATIONAL RESCUE!
THREE MILES NORTH OF MOUNT VESUVIUS, SCOTT. MARATHON RUNNERS TRAPPED ON A LEDGE. THE DISTRESS CALL IS FOR SPEED, SPEED AND MORE SPEED!
TB1
THUNDERBIRD ONE... TOUCHDOWN ITALY!
INTERNATIONAL RESCUE. ARE THOSE TWO GUYS STILL ALIVE?
THAT, SIGNOR, IS WHAT WE DO NOT KNOW. TEN MINUTES AGO, THEY VANISHED FROM THE LEDGE...
ONE MOMENT THEY WERE THERE, AND THE NEXT... THEY WERE GONE!
I'LL GO DOWN AND HAVE A LOOK.
USING HIS COMPACT THRUST PACK, SCOTT SAILS DOWN THE CLIFF FACE...
A CAVE... SO THAT'S IT! THEY PROBABLY CRAWLED IN THERE WHEN THEY RECOVERED CONSCIOUSNESS.
BALDWIN! ZELGAD! WHAT THE...?

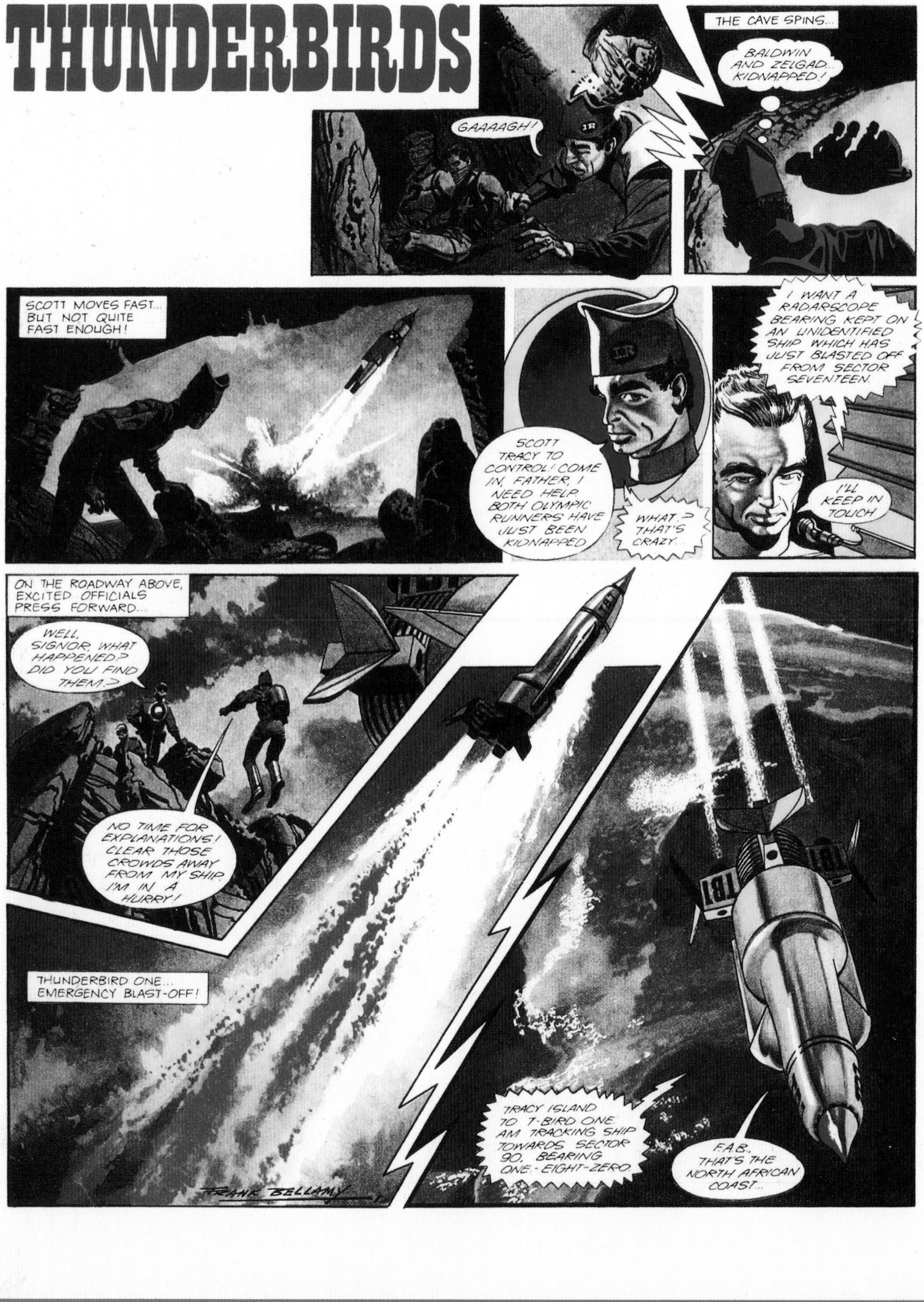
THUNDERBIRDS
THE CAVE SPINS...
BALDWIN AND ZELGAD... KIDNAPPED!
GAAAAGH!
SCOTT MOVES FAST... BUT NOT QUITE FAST ENOUGH!
SCOTT TRACY TO CONTROL! COME IN, FATHER, I NEED HELP. BOTH OLYMPIC RUNNERS HAVE JUST BEEN KIDNAPPED
WHAT?! THAT'S CRAZY...
I WANT A RADARSCOPE BEARING KEPT ON AN UNIDENTIFIED SHIP WHICH HAS JUST BLASTED OFF FROM SECTOR SEVENTEEN.
I'LL KEEP IN TOUCH.
ON THE ROADWAY ABOVE, EXCITED OFFICIALS PRESS FORWARD...
WELL, SIGNOR, WHAT HAPPENED? DID YOU FIND THEM?
NO TIME FOR EXPLANATIONS! CLEAR THOSE CROWDS AWAY FROM MY SHIP. I'M IN A HURRY!
THUNDERBIRD ONE... EMERGENCY BLAST-OFF!
TRACY ISLAND TO T-BIRD ONE. AM TRACKING SHIP TOWARDS SECTOR 90. BEARING ONE-EIGHT-ZERO.
F.A.B.. THAT'S THE NORTH AFRICAN COAST...
FRANK BELLAMY

Artist: Frank Bellamy

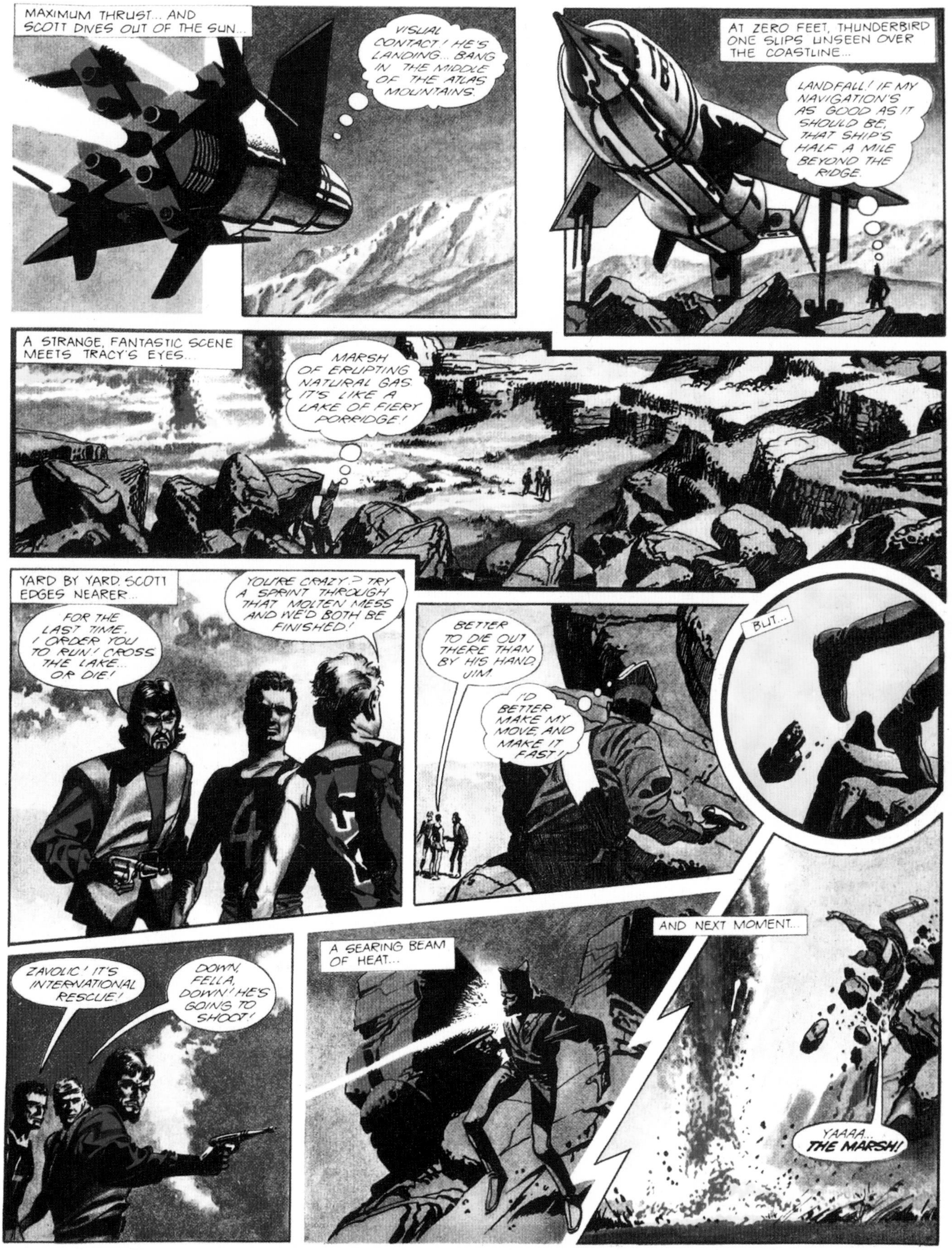
MAXIMUM THRUST... AND SCOTT DIVES OUT OF THE SUN...
VISUAL CONTACT! HE'S LANDING... BANG IN THE MIDDLE OF THE ATLAS MOUNTAINS.
AT ZERO FEET, THUNDERBIRD ONE SLIPS UNSEEN OVER THE COASTLINE...
TB1
LANDFALL! IF MY NAVIGATION'S AS GOOD AS IT SHOULD BE, THAT SHIP'S HALF A MILE BEYOND THE RIDGE.
A STRANGE, FANTASTIC SCENE MEETS TRACY'S EYES...
MARSH OF ERUPTING NATURAL GAS. IT'S LIKE A LAKE OF FIERY PORRIDGE!
YARD BY YARD, SCOTT EDGES NEARER...
FOR THE LAST TIME, I ORDER YOU TO RUN! CROSS THE LAKE... OR DIE!
YOU'RE CRAZY.' TRY A SPRINT THROUGH THAT MOLTEN MESS AND WE'D BOTH BE FINISHED!
BETTER TO DIE OUT THERE THAN BY HIS HAND, JIM.
I'D BETTER MAKE MY MOVE, AND MAKE IT FAST!
BUT...
ZAVOLIC! IT'S INTERNATIONAL RESCUE!
DOWN, FELLA, DOWN! HE'S GOING TO SHOOT!
A SEARING BEAM OF HEAT...
AND NEXT MOMENT...
YAAAA... THE MARSH!

Part 3 - adteline 25 May 2068

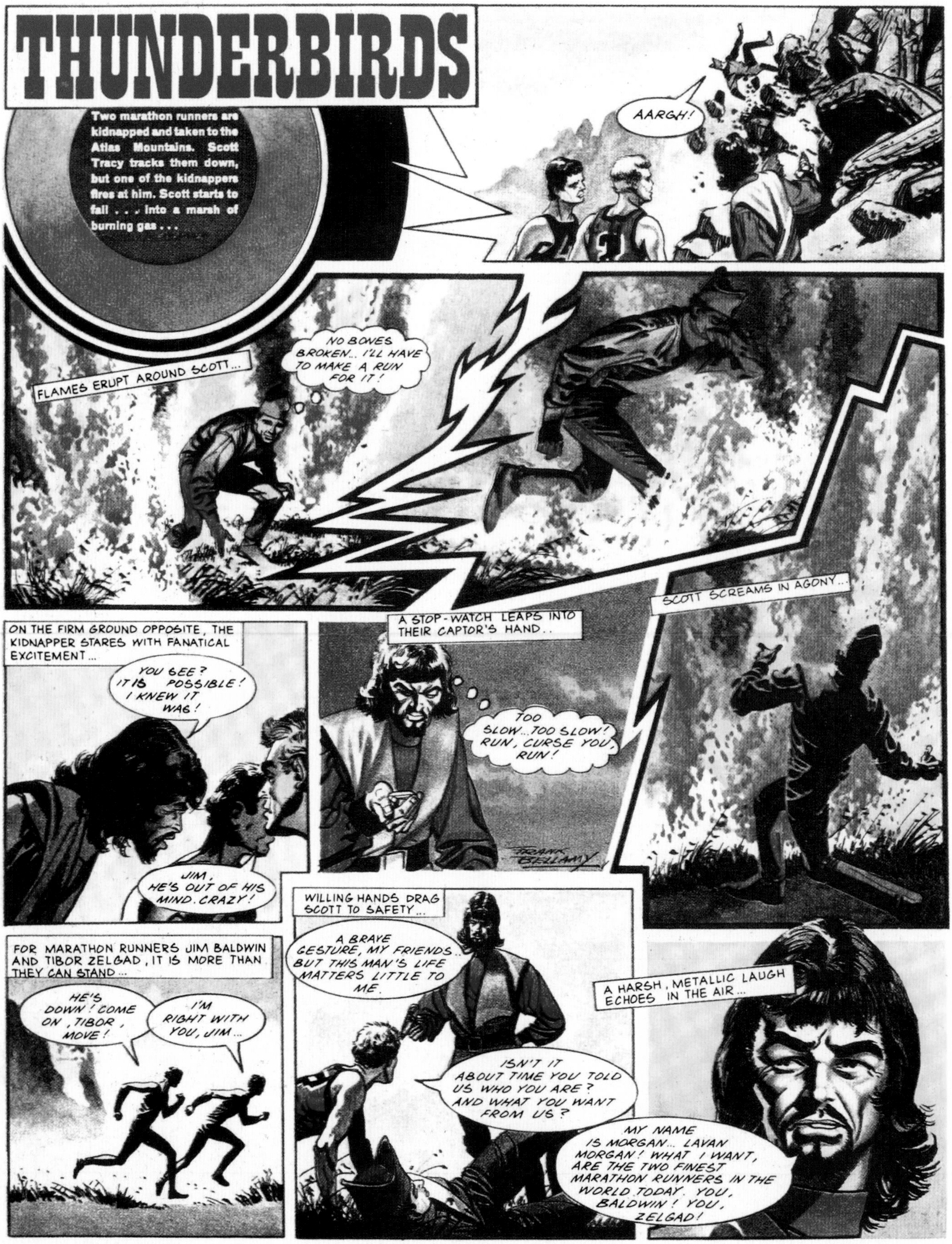
THUNDERBIRDS
Two marathon runners are kidnapped and taken to the Atlas Mountains. Scott Tracy tracks them down, but one of the kidnappers fires at him. Scott starts to fall . . . into a marsh of burning gas . . .
AARGH!
FLAMES ERUPT AROUND SCOTT...
NO BONES BROKEN... I'LL HAVE TO MAKE A RUN FOR IT!
ON THE FIRM GROUND OPPOSITE, THE KIDNAPPER STARES WITH FANATICAL EXCITEMENT...
YOU SEE? IT IS POSSIBLE! I KNEW IT WAS!
JIM, HE'S OUT OF HIS MIND. CRAZY!
A STOP-WATCH LEAPS INTO THEIR CAPTOR'S HAND..
TOO SLOW...TOO SLOW! RUN, CURSE YOU, RUN!
FRANK BELLAMY
SCOTT SCREAMS IN AGONY...
FOR MARATHON RUNNERS JIM BALDWIN AND TIBOR ZELGAD, IT IS MORE THAN THEY CAN STAND...
HE'S DOWN! COME ON, TIBOR, MOVE!
I'M RIGHT WITH YOU, JIM...
WILLING HANDS DRAG SCOTT TO SAFETY...
A BRAVE GESTURE, MY FRIENDS.. BUT THIS MAN'S LIFE MATTERS LITTLE TO ME.
ISN'T IT ABOUT TIME YOU TOLD US WHO YOU ARE? AND WHAT YOU WANT FROM US?
A HARSH, METALLIC LAUGH ECHOES IN THE AIR...
MY NAME IS MORGAN... LAVAN MORGAN! WHAT I WANT, ARE THE TWO FINEST MARATHON RUNNERS IN THE WORLD TODAY. YOU, BALDWIN! YOU, ZELGAD!

Artist: Frank Bellamy

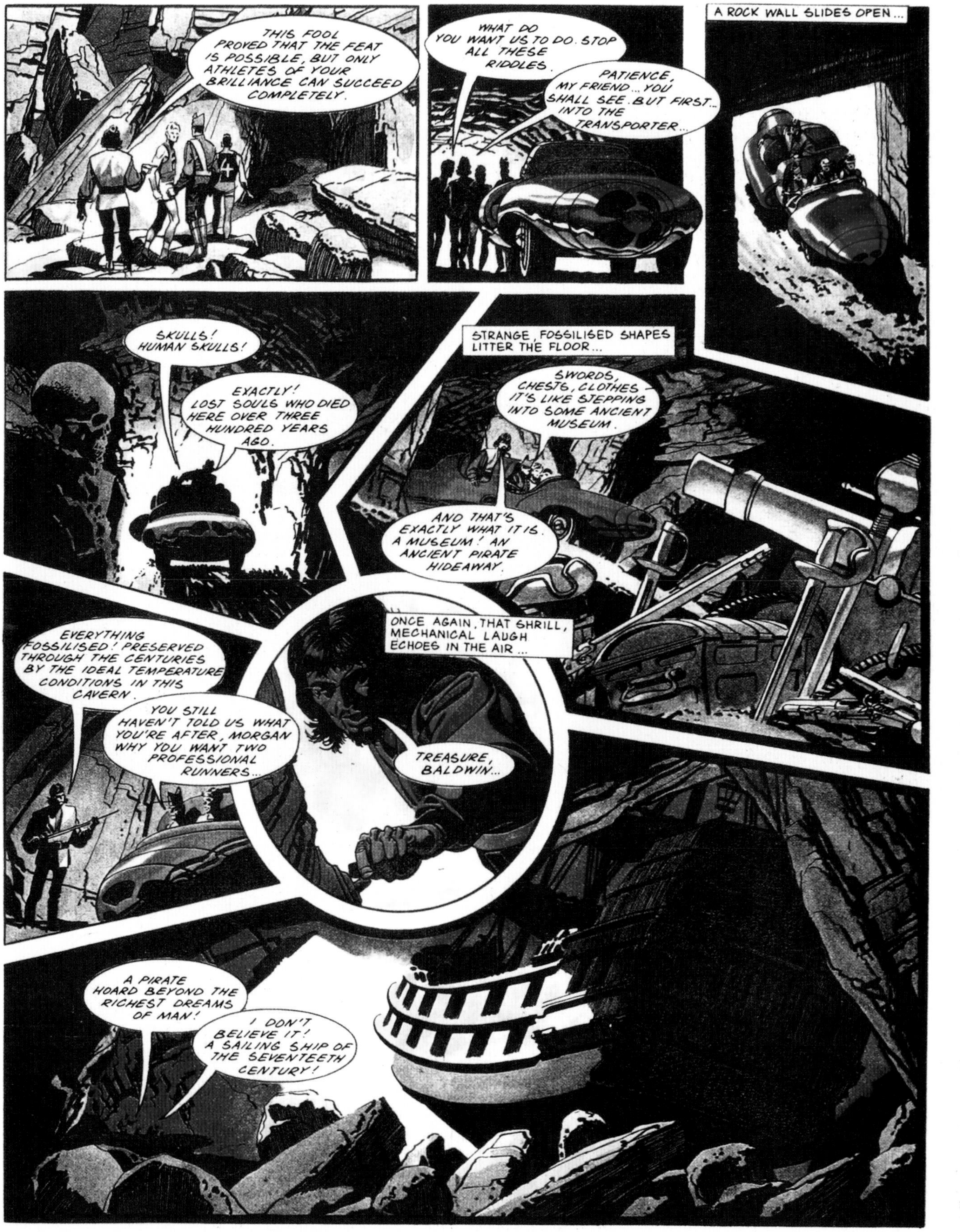
THIS FOOL PROVED THAT THE FEAT IS POSSIBLE, BUT ONLY ATHLETES OF YOUR BRILLIANCE CAN SUCCEED COMPLETELY.
WHAT DO YOU WANT US TO DO. STOP ALL THESE RIDDLES.
PATIENCE, MY FRIEND... YOU SHALL SEE. BUT FIRST... INTO THE TRANSPORTER...
A ROCK WALL SLIDES OPEN...
SKULLS! HUMAN SKULLS!
EXACTLY! LOST SOULS WHO DIED HERE OVER THREE HUNDRED YEARS AGO.
STRANGE, FOSSILISED SHAPES LITTER THE FLOOR...
SWORDS, CHESTS, CLOTHES - IT'S LIKE STEPPING INTO SOME ANCIENT MUSEUM.
AND THAT'S EXACTLY WHAT IT IS. A MUSEUM! AN ANCIENT PIRATE HIDEAWAY.
EVERYTHING FOSSILISED! PRESERVED THROUGH THE CENTURIES BY THE IDEAL TEMPERATURE CONDITIONS IN THIS CAVERN.
YOU STILL HAVEN'T TOLD US WHAT YOU'RE AFTER, MORGAN WHY YOU WANT TWO PROFESSIONAL RUNNERS...
ONCE AGAIN, THAT SHRILL, MECHANICAL LAUGH ECHOES IN THE AIR...
TREASURE, BALDWIN...
A PIRATE HOARD BEYOND THE RICHEST DREAMS OF MAN!
I DON'T BELIEVE IT! A SAILING SHIP OF THE SEVENTEETH CENTURY!

Part 4 - dateline 01 June 2068

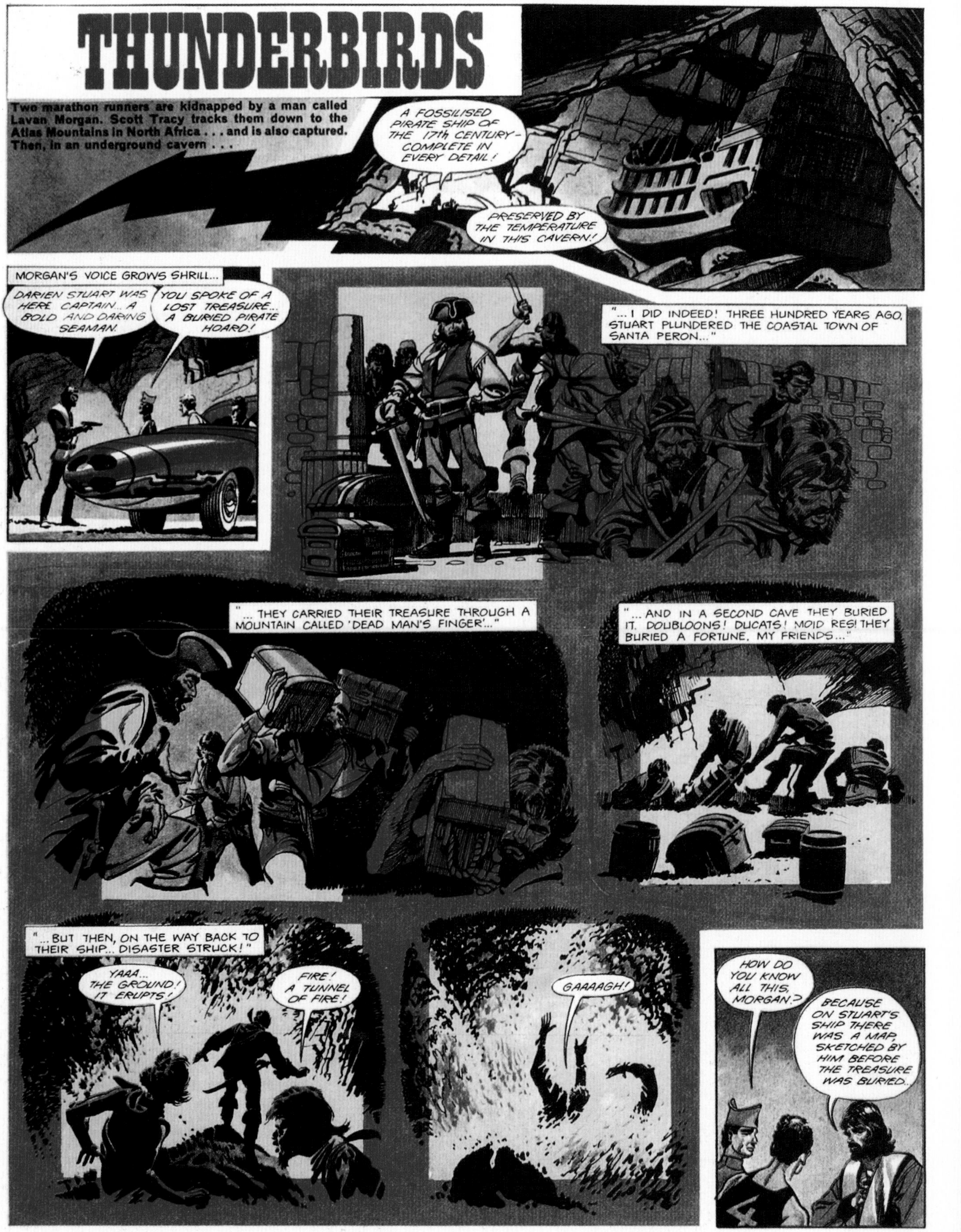
THUNDERBIRDS
Two marathon runners are kidnapped by a man called Lavan Morgan. Scott Tracy tracks them down to the Atlas Mountains in North Africa . . . and is also captured. Then, in an underground cavern . . .
A FOSSILISED PIRATE SHIP OF THE 17th CENTURY - COMPLETE IN EVERY DETAIL!
PRESERVED BY THE TEMPERATURE IN THIS CAVERN!
MORGAN'S VOICE GROWS SHRILL...
DARIEN STUART WAS HERE CAPTAIN... A BOLD AND DARING SEAMAN.
YOU SPOKE OF A LOST TREASURE... A BURIED PIRATE HOARD!
"... I DID INDEED! THREE HUNDRED YEARS AGO, STUART PLUNDERED THE COASTAL TOWN OF SANTA PERON..."
"... THEY CARRIED THEIR TREASURE THROUGH A MOUNTAIN CALLED 'DEAD MAN'S FINGER'..."
"... AND IN A SECOND CAVE THEY BURIED IT. DOUBLOONS! DUCATS! MOID RES! THEY BURIED A FORTUNE, MY FRIENDS..."
"... BUT THEN, ON THE WAY BACK TO THEIR SHIP... DISASTER STRUCK!"
YAAA... THE GROUND! IT ERUPTS!
FIRE! A TUNNEL OF FIRE!
GAAAAGH!
HOW DO YOU KNOW ALL THIS, MORGAN?
BECAUSE ON STUART'S SHIP THERE WAS A MAP, SKETCHED BY HIM BEFORE THE TREASURE WAS BURIED...

Artist: Frank Bellamy

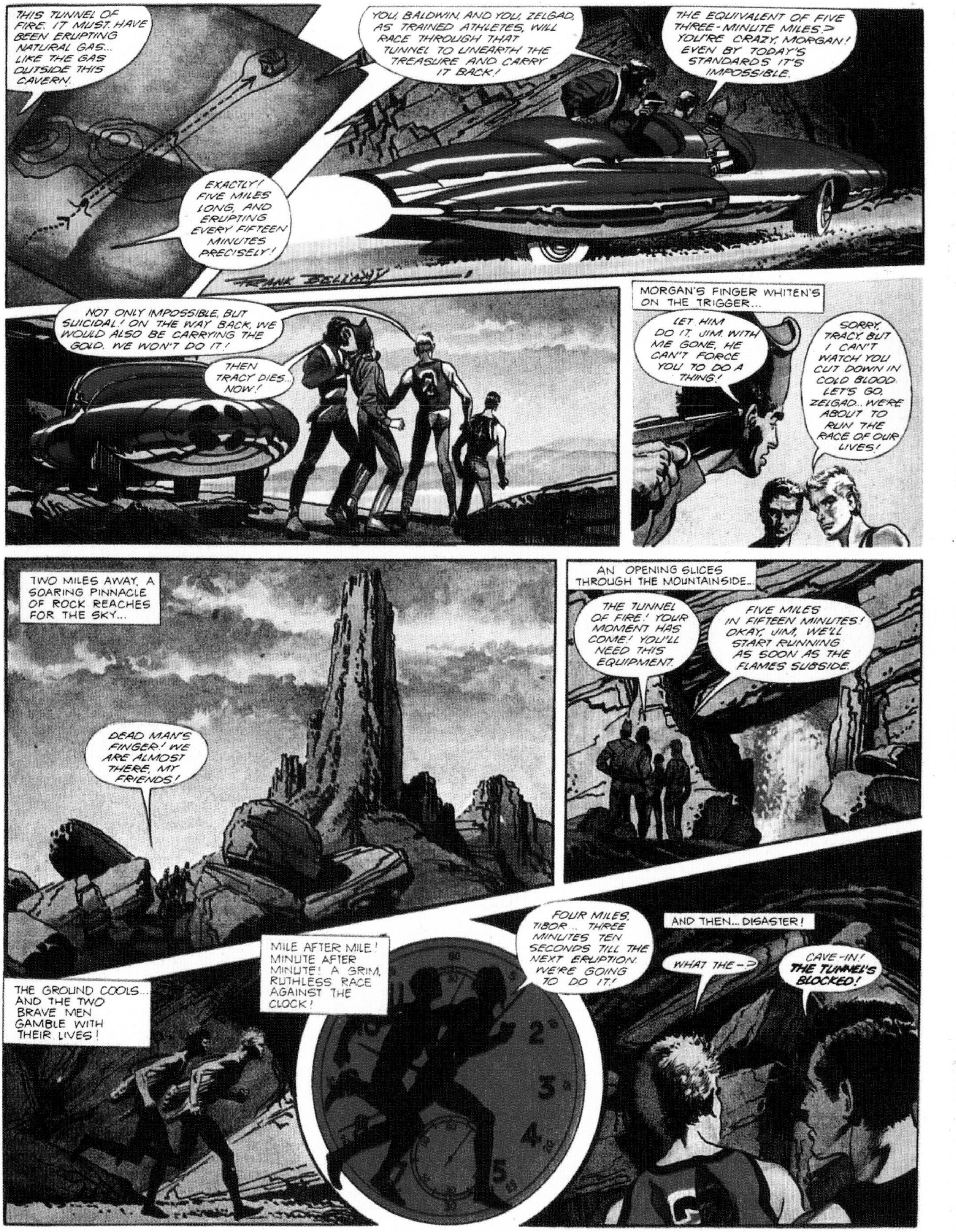
THIS TUNNEL OF FIRE. IT MUST HAVE BEEN ERUPTING NATURAL GAS... LIKE THE GAS OUTSIDE THIS CAVERN.
YOU, BALDWIN, AND YOU, ZELGAD, AS TRAINED ATHLETES, WILL RACE THROUGH THAT TUNNEL TO UNEARTH THE TREASURE AND CARRY IT BACK!
THE EQUIVALENT OF FIVE THREE-MINUTE MILES? YOU'RE CRAZY, MORGAN! EVEN BY TODAY'S STANDARDS IT'S IMPOSSIBLE.
EXACTLY! FIVE MILES LONG, AND ERUPTING EVERY FIFTEEN MINUTES PRECISELY!
FRANK BELLAMY
NOT ONLY IMPOSSIBLE, BUT SUICIDAL! ON THE WAY BACK, WE WOULD ALSO BE CARRYING THE GOLD. WE WON'T DO IT!
THEN TRACY DIES... NOW!
MORGAN'S FINGER WHITEN'S ON THE TRIGGER...
LET HIM DO IT, JIM. WITH ME GONE, HE CAN'T FORCE YOU TO DO A THING!
SORRY, TRACY, BUT I CAN'T WATCH YOU CUT DOWN IN COLD BLOOD. LET'S GO, ZELGAD... WE'RE ABOUT TO RUN THE RACE OF OUR LIVES!
TWO MILES AWAY, A SOARING PINNACLE OF ROCK REACHES FOR THE SKY...
DEAD MAN'S FINGER! WE ARE ALMOST THERE, MY FRIENDS!
AN OPENING SLICES THROUGH THE MOUNTAINSIDE...
THE TUNNEL OF FIRE! YOUR MOMENT HAS COME! YOU'LL NEED THIS EQUIPMENT.
FIVE MILES IN FIFTEEN MINUTES! OKAY, JIM, WE'LL START RUNNING AS SOON AS THE FLAMES SUBSIDE.
THE GROUND COOLS... AND THE TWO BRAVE MEN GAMBLE WITH THEIR LIVES!
MILE AFTER MILE! MINUTE AFTER MINUTE! A GRIM, RUTHLESS RACE AGAINST THE CLOCK!
FOUR MILES, TIBOR... THREE MINUTES TEN SECONDS TILL THE NEXT ERUPTION. WE'RE GOING TO DO IT!
AND THEN... DISASTER!
WHAT THE-?
CAVE-IN! THE TUNNEL'S BLOCKED!

Part 5 - dateline 08 June 2068

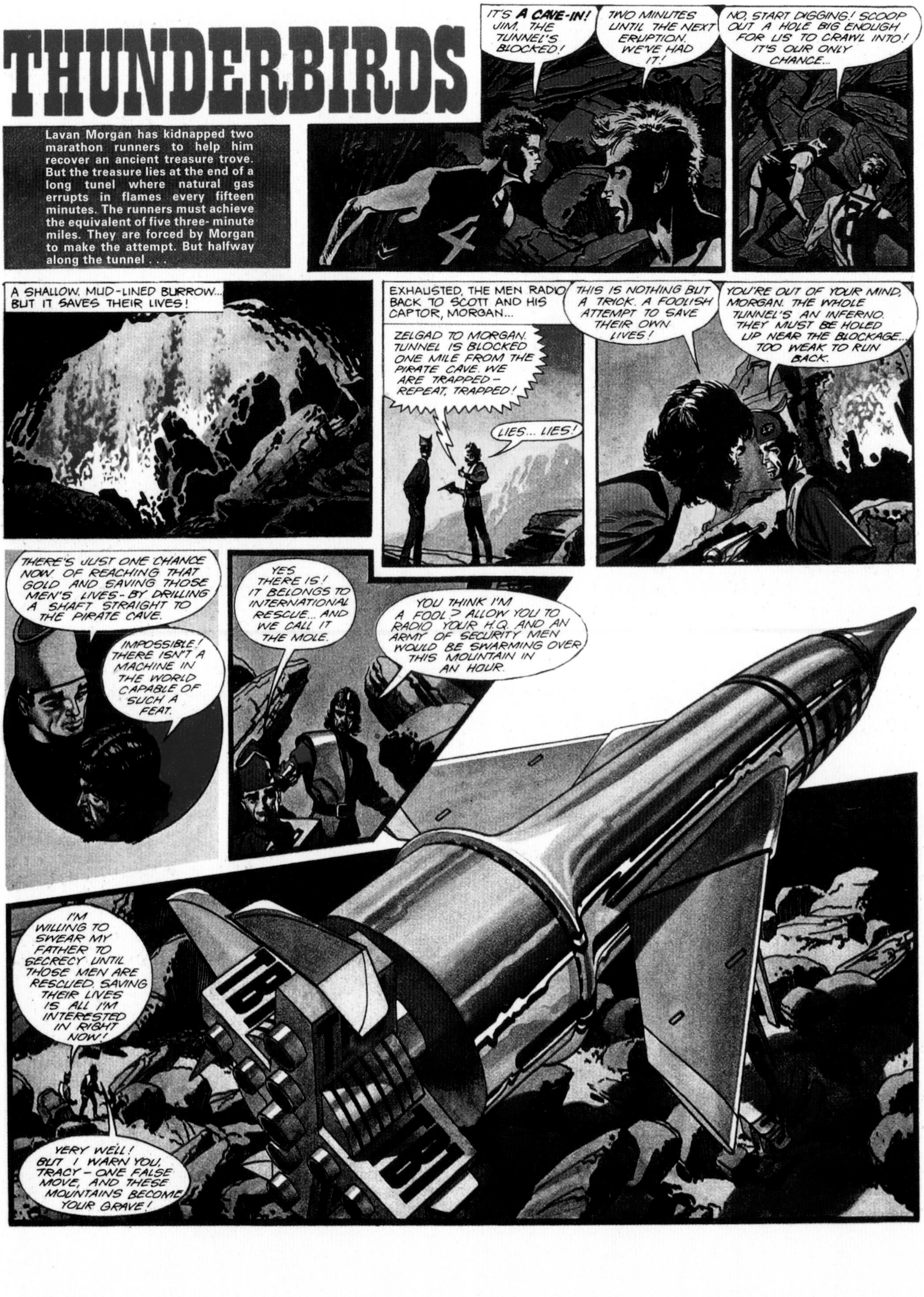
THUNDERBIRDS
Lavan Morgan has kidnapped two marathon runners to help him recover an ancient treasure trove. But the treasure lies at the end of a long tunel where natural gas errupts in flames every fifteen minutes. The runners must achieve the equivalent of five three- minute miles. They are forced by Morgan to make the attempt. But halfway along the tunnel . . .
IT'S A CAVE-IN! JIM, THE TUNNEL'S BLOCKED!
TWO MINUTES UNTIL THE NEXT ERUPTION. WE'VE HAD IT!
NO, START DIGGING! SCOOP OUT A HOLE BIG ENOUGH FOR US TO CRAWL INTO! IT'S OUR ONLY CHANCE...
A SHALLOW, MUD-LINED BURROW... BUT IT SAVES THEIR LIVES!
EXHAUSTED, THE MEN RADIO BACK TO SCOTT AND HIS CAPTOR, MORGAN...
ZELGAD TO MORGAN. TUNNEL IS BLOCKED ONE MILE FROM THE PIRATE CAVE. WE ARE TRAPPED - REPEAT, TRAPPED!
LIES... LIES!
THIS IS NOTHING BUT A TRICK. A FOOLISH ATTEMPT TO SAVE THEIR OWN LIVES!
YOU'RE OUT OF YOUR MIND, MORGAN. THE WHOLE TUNNEL'S AN INFERNO. THEY MUST BE HOLED UP NEAR THE BLOCKAGE... TOO WEAK TO RUN BACK.
THERE'S JUST ONE CHANCE NOW OF REACHING THAT GOLD AND SAVING THOSE MEN'S LIVES - BY DRILLING A SHAFT STRAIGHT TO THE PIRATE CAVE.
IMPOSSIBLE! THERE ISN'T A MACHINE IN THE WORLD CAPABLE OF SUCH A FEAT.
YES THERE IS! IT BELONGS TO INTERNATIONAL RESCUE... AND WE CALL IT THE MOLE.
YOU THINK I'M A FOOL? ALLOW YOU TO RADIO YOUR H.Q. AND AN ARMY OF SECURITY MEN WOULD BE SWARMING OVER THIS MOUNTAIN IN AN HOUR.
I'M WILLING TO SWEAR MY FATHER TO SECRECY UNTIL THOSE MEN ARE RESCUED. SAVING THEIR LIVES IS ALL I'M INTERESTED IN RIGHT NOW!
VERY WELL! BUT I WARN YOU, TRACY - ONE FALSE MOVE, AND THESE MOUNTAINS BECOME YOUR GRAVE!
TB1

Artist: Frank Bellamy

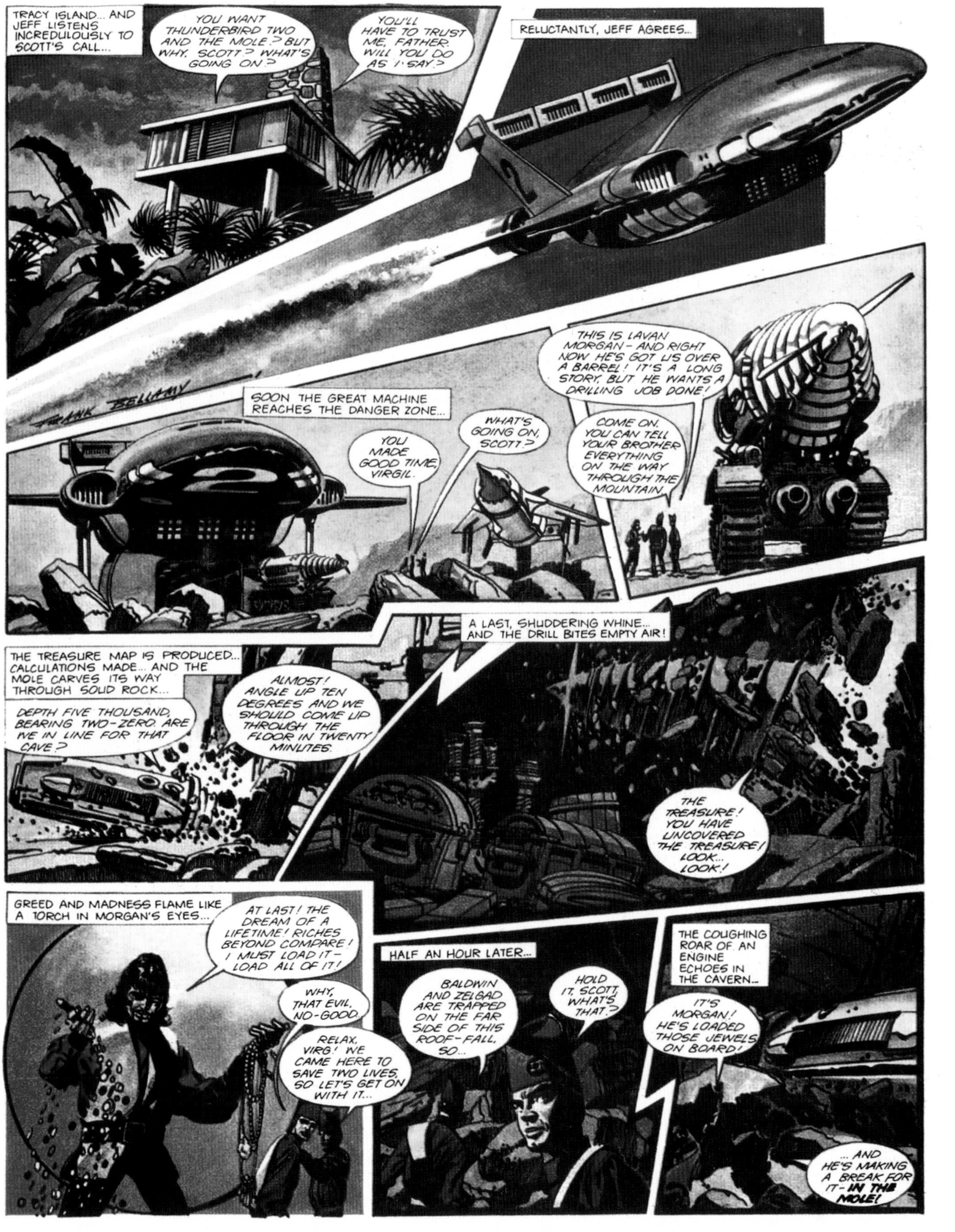
TRACY ISLAND... AND JEFF LISTENS INCREDULOUSLY TO SCOTT'S CALL...
YOU WANT THUNDERBIRD TWO AND THE MOLE? BUT WHY, SCOTT? WHAT'S GOING ON?
YOU'LL HAVE TO TRUST ME, FATHER. WILL YOU DO AS I SAY?
RELUCTANTLY, JEFF AGREES...
FRANK BELLAMY
SOON THE GREAT MACHINE REACHES THE DANGER ZONE...
YOU MADE GOOD TIME, VIRGIL.
WHAT'S GOING ON, SCOTT?
THIS IS LAVAN MORGAN - AND RIGHT NOW HE'S GOT US OVER A BARREL! IT'S A LONG STORY, BUT HE WANTS A DRILLING JOB DONE!
COME ON. YOU CAN TELL YOUR BROTHER EVERYTHING ON THE WAY THROUGH THE MOUNTAIN.
THE TREASURE MAP IS PRODUCED... CALCULATIONS MADE... AND THE MOLE CARVES ITS WAY THROUGH SOLID ROCK...
DEPTH FIVE THOUSAND, BEARING TWO-ZERO. ARE WE IN LINE FOR THAT CAVE?
ALMOST! ANGLE UP TEN DEGREES AND WE SHOULD COME UP THROUGH THE FLOOR IN TWENTY MINUTES.
A LAST, SHUDDERING WHINE... AND THE DRILL BITES EMPTY AIR!
THE TREASURE! YOU HAVE UNCOVERED THE TREASURE! LOOK... LOOK!
GREED AND MADNESS FLAME LIKE A TORCH IN MORGAN'S EYES...
AT LAST! THE DREAM OF A LIFETIME! RICHES BEYOND COMPARE! I MUST LOAD IT - LOAD ALL OF IT!
WHY, THAT EVIL, NO-GOOD...
RELAX, VIRG! WE CAME HERE TO SAVE TWO LIVES, SO LET'S GET ON WITH IT...
HALF AN HOUR LATER...
BALDWIN AND ZELGAD ARE TRAPPED ON THE FAR SIDE OF THIS ROOF-FALL, SO...
HOLD IT, SCOTT, WHAT'S THAT?
THE COUGHING ROAR OF AN ENGINE ECHOES IN THE CAVERN...
IT'S MORGAN! HE'S LOADED THOSE JEWELS ON BOARD!
... AND HE'S MAKING A BREAK FOR IT - IN THE MOLE!

Part 6 - dateline 15 June 2068

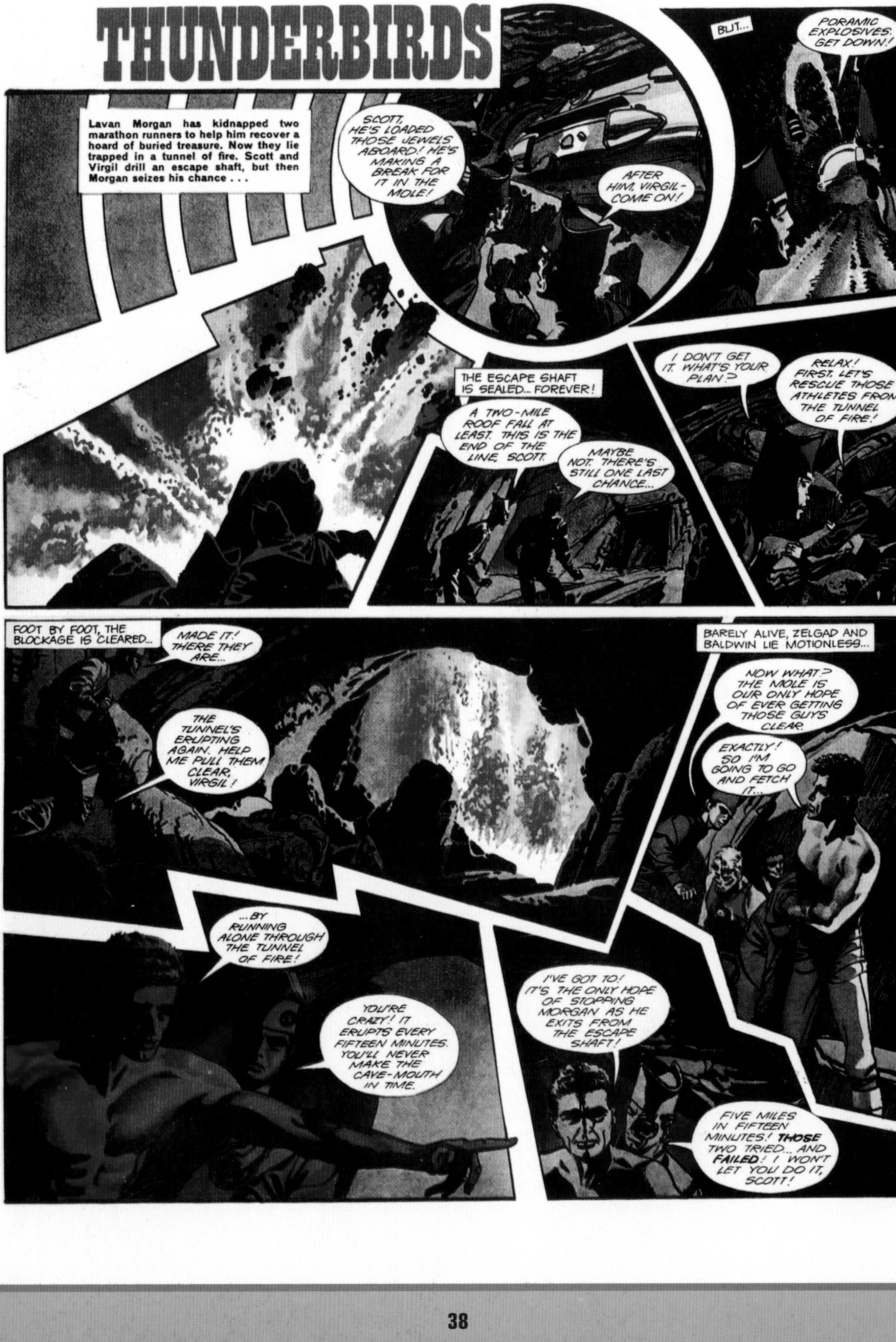
THUNDERBIRDS
Lavan Morgan has kidnapped two marathon runners to help him recover a hoard of buried treasure. Now they lie trapped in a tunnel of fire. Scott and Virgil drill an escape shaft, but then Morgan seizes his chance . . .
SCOTT, HE'S LOADED THOSE JEWELS ABOARD! HE'S MAKING A BREAK FOR IT IN THE MOLE!
AFTER HIM, VIRGIL-COME ON!
BUT...
PORAMIC EXPLOSIVES! GET DOWN!
THE ESCAPE SHAFT IS SEALED... FOREVER!
A TWO-MILE ROOF FALL AT LEAST. THIS IS THE END OF THE LINE, SCOTT.
MAYBE NOT. THERE'S STILL ONE LAST CHANCE...
I DON'T GET IT. WHAT'S YOUR PLAN?
RELAX! FIRST, LET'S RESCUE THOSE ATHLETES FROM THE TUNNEL OF FIRE!
FOOT BY FOOT, THE BLOCKAGE IS CLEARED...
MADE IT! THERE THEY ARE...
THE TUNNEL'S ERUPTING AGAIN. HELP ME PULL THEM CLEAR, VIRGIL!
BARELY ALIVE, ZELGAD AND BALDWIN LIE MOTIONLESS...
NOW WHAT? THE MOLE IS OUR ONLY HOPE OF EVER GETTING THOSE GUYS CLEAR.
EXACTLY! SO I'M GOING TO GO AND FETCH IT...
...BY RUNNING ALONE THROUGH THE TUNNEL OF FIRE!
YOU'RE CRAZY! IT ERUPTS EVERY FIFTEEN MINUTES. YOU'LL NEVER MAKE THE CAVE-MOUTH IN TIME.
I'VE GOT TO! IT'S THE ONLY HOPE OF STOPPING MORGAN AS HE EXITS FROM THE ESCAPE SHAFT!
FIVE MILES IN FIFTEEN MINUTES! THOSE TWO TRIED... AND FAILED! I WON'T LET YOU DO IT, SCOTT!

Artist: Frank Bellamy

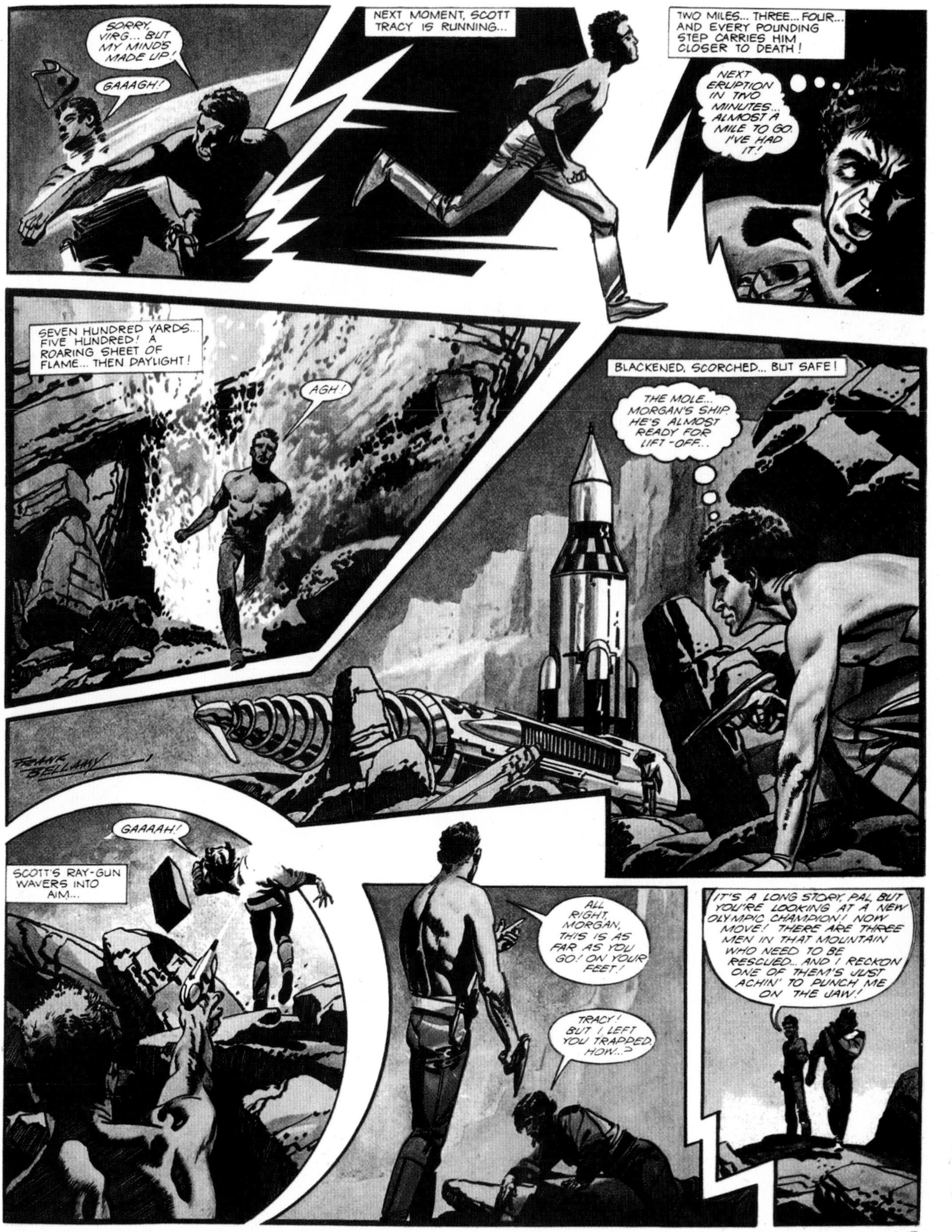
SORRY, VIRG... BUT MY MIND'S MADE UP!
GAAAGH!
NEXT MOMENT, SCOTT TRACY IS RUNNING...
TWO MILES... THREE... FOUR... AND EVERY POUNDING STEP CARRIES HIM CLOSER TO DEATH!
NEXT ERUPTION IN TWO MINUTES... ALMOST A MILE TO GO. I'VE HAD IT!
SEVEN HUNDRED YARDS... FIVE HUNDRED! A ROARING SHEET OF FLAME... THEN DAYLIGHT!
AGH!
BLACKENED, SCORCHED... BUT SAFE!
THE MOLE... MORGAN'S SHIP. HE'S ALMOST READY FOR LIFT-OFF...
FRANK BELLAMY
GAAAAH!
SCOTT'S RAY-GUN WAVERS INTO AIM...
ALL RIGHT, MORGAN, THIS IS AS FAR AS YOU GO! ON YOUR FEET!
TRACY! BUT I, LEFT YOU TRAPPED. HOW..?
IT'S A LONG STORY, PAL, BUT YOU'RE LOOKING AT A NEW OLYMPIC CHAMPION! NOW MOVE! THERE ARE THREE MEN IN THAT MOUNTAIN WHO NEED TO BE RESCUED... AND I RECKON ONE OF THEM'S JUST ACHIN' TO PUNCH ME ON THE JAW!

Part 1 - dateline 27 July 2068

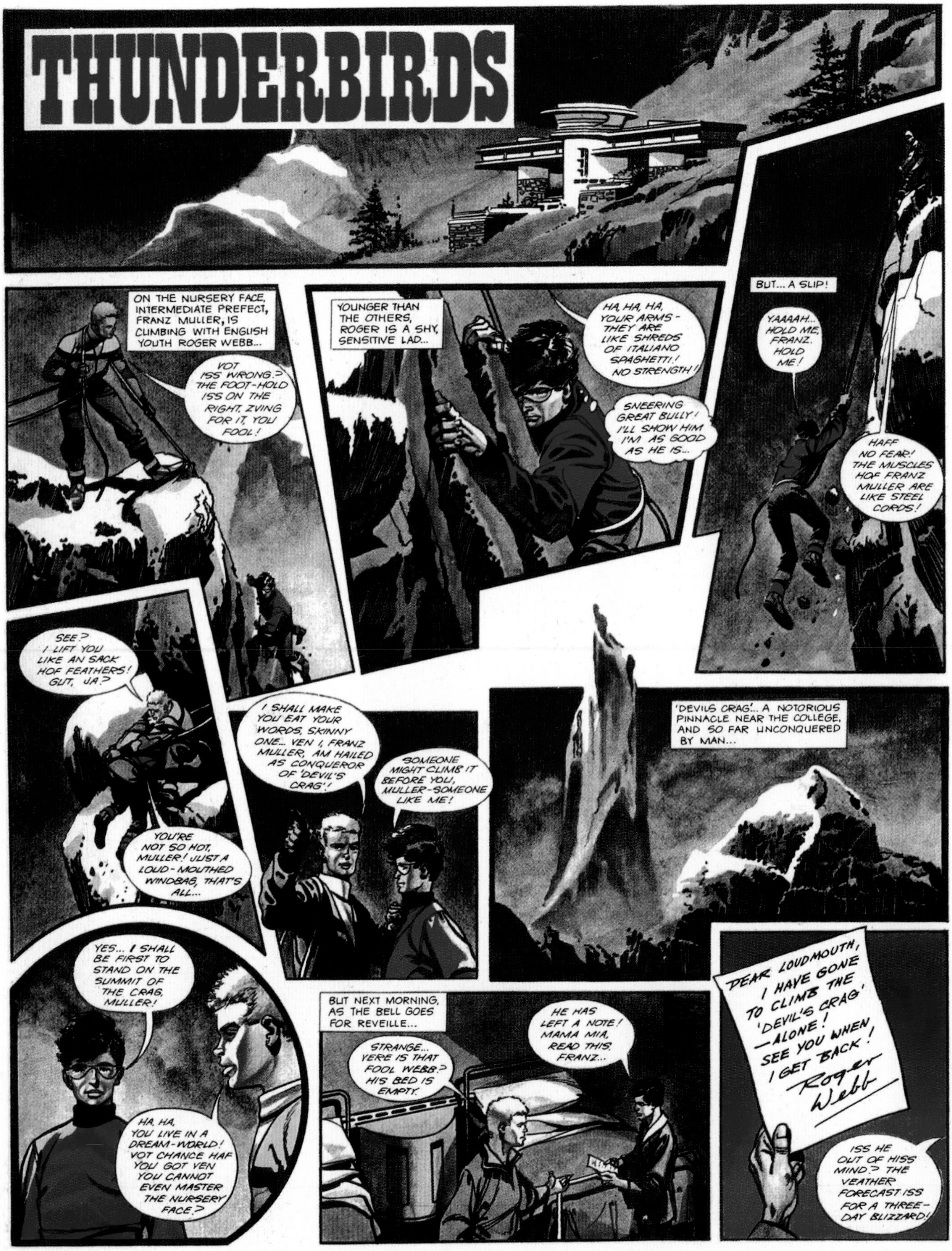
THUNDERBIRDS
ON THE NURSERY FACE, INTERMEDIATE PREFECT, FRANZ MULLER, IS CLIMBING WITH ENGLISH YOUTH ROGER WEBB...
VOT ISS WRONG? THE FOOT-HOLD ISS ON THE RIGHT, ZVING FOR IT, YOU FOOL!
YOUNGER THAN THE OTHERS, ROGER IS A SHY, SENSITIVE LAD...
HA, HA, HA, YOUR ARMS - THEY ARE LIKE SHREDS OF ITALIANO SPAGHETTI! NO STRENGTH!
SNEERING GREAT BULLY! I'LL SHOW HIM I'M AS GOOD AS HE IS...
BUT... A SLIP!
YAAAAH... HOLD ME, FRANZ. HOLD ME!
HAFF NO FEAR! THE MUSCLES HOF FRANZ MULLER ARE LIKE STEEL CORDS!
SEE? I LIFT YOU LIKE AN SACK HOF FEATHERS! GUT, JA?
YOU'RE NOT SO HOT, MULLER! JUST A LOUD-MOUTHED WINDBAG, THAT'S ALL...
I SHALL MAKE YOU EAT YOUR WORDS, SKINNY ONE... VEN I, FRANZ MULLER, AM HAILED AS CONQUEROR OF 'DEVIL'S CRAG'!
SOMEONE MIGHT CLIMB IT BEFORE YOU, MULLER-SOMEONE LIKE ME!
'DEVILS CRAG'... A NOTORIOUS PINNACLE NEAR THE COLLEGE, AND SO FAR UNCONQUERED BY MAN...
YES... I SHALL BE FIRST TO STAND ON THE SUMMIT OF THE CRAG, MULLER!
HA, HA, YOU LIVE IN A DREAM-WORLD! VOT CHANCE HAF YOU GOT VEN YOU CANNOT EVEN MASTER THE NURSERY FACE?
BUT NEXT MORNING, AS THE BELL GOES FOR REVEILLE...
STRANGE... YERE IS THAT FOOL WEBB? HIS BED IS EMPTY.
HE HAS LEFT A NOTE! MAMA MIA, READ THIS, FRANZ...
DEAR LOUDMOUTH, I HAVE GONE TO CLIMB THE 'DEVIL'S CRAG' —ALONE! SEE YOU WHEN I GET BACK! Roger Webb
ISS HE OUT OF HISS MIND? THE VEATHER FORECAST ISS FOR A THREE-DAY BLIZZARD!

Artist: Frank Bellamy

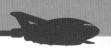

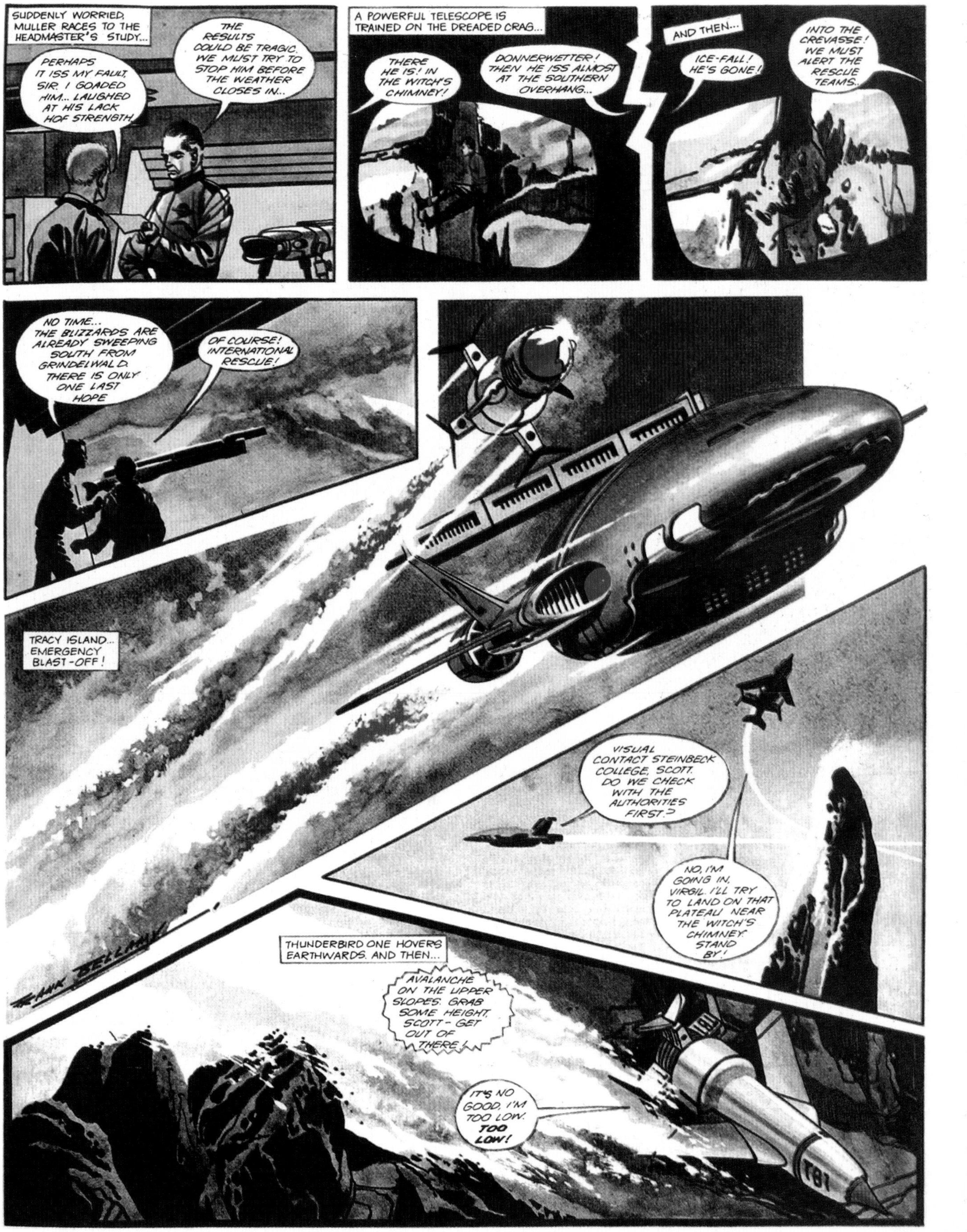
SUDDENLY WORRIED, MULLER RACES TO THE HEADMASTER'S STUDY...
PERHAPS IT ISS MY FAULT, SIR. I GOADED HIM... LAUGHED AT HIS LACK HOF STRENGTH.
THE RESULTS COULD BE TRAGIC. WE MUST TRY TO STOP HIM BEFORE THE WEATHER CLOSES IN...
A POWERFUL TELESCOPE IS TRAINED ON THE DREADED CRAG...
THERE HE IS! IN THE WITCH'S CHIMNEY!
DONNERWETTER! THEN HE ISS ALMOST AT THE SOUTHERN OVERHANG...
AND THEN...
ICE-FALL! HE'S GONE!
INTO THE CREVASSE! WE MUST ALERT THE RESCUE TEAMS...
NO TIME... THE BLIZZARDS ARE ALREADY SWEEPING SOUTH FROM GRINDELWALD. THERE IS ONLY ONE LAST HOPE
OF COURSE! INTERNATIONAL RESCUE!
TRACY ISLAND... EMERGENCY BLAST-OFF!
VISUAL CONTACT STEINBECK COLLEGE, SCOTT. DO WE CHECK WITH THE AUTHORITIES FIRST?
NO, I'M GOING IN, VIRGIL. I'LL TRY TO LAND ON THAT PLATEAU NEAR THE WITCH'S CHIMNEY. STAND BY!
THUNDERBIRD ONE HOVERS EARTHWARDS. AND THEN...
AVALANCHE ON THE UPPER SLOPES. GRAB SOME HEIGHT, SCOTT - GET OUT OF THERE!
IT'S NO GOOD, I'M TOO LOW. TOO LOW!

Part 2 - adteline 03 August 2068

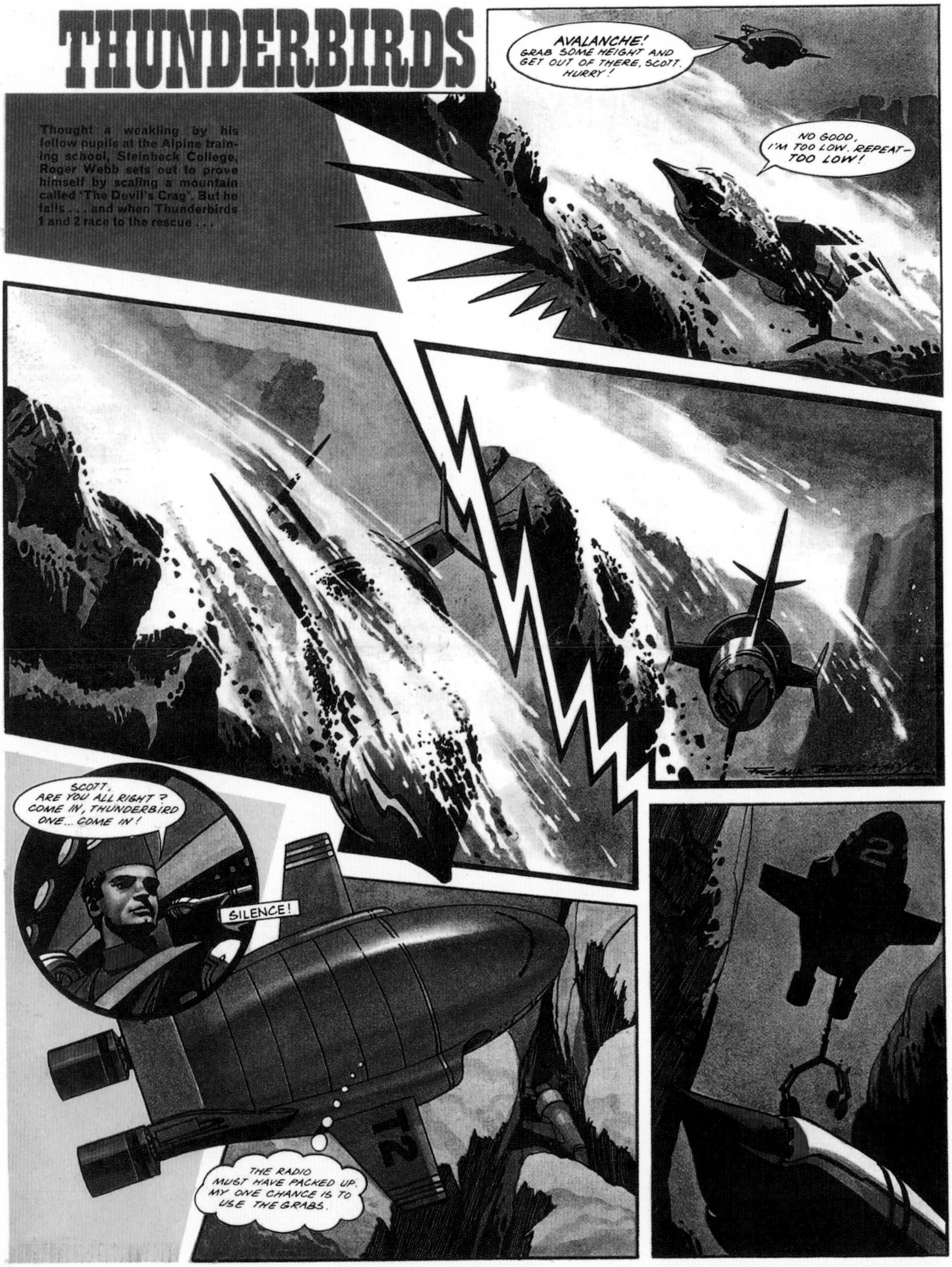
THUNDERBIRDS
Thought a weakling by his fellow pupils at the Alpine training school, Steinbeck College, Roger Webb sets out to prove himself by scaling a mountain called 'The Devil's Crag'. But he falls . . . and when Thunderbirds 1 and 2 race to the rescue . . .
AVALANCHE! GRAB SOME HEIGHT AND GET OUT OF THERE, SCOTT. HURRY!
NO GOOD, I'M TOO LOW. REPEAT— TOO LOW!
SCOTT, ARE YOU ALL RIGHT? COME IN, THUNDERBIRD ONE... COME IN!
SILENCE!
THE RADIO MUST HAVE PACKED UP. MY ONE CHANCE IS TO USE THE GRABS.

Artist: Frank Bellamy

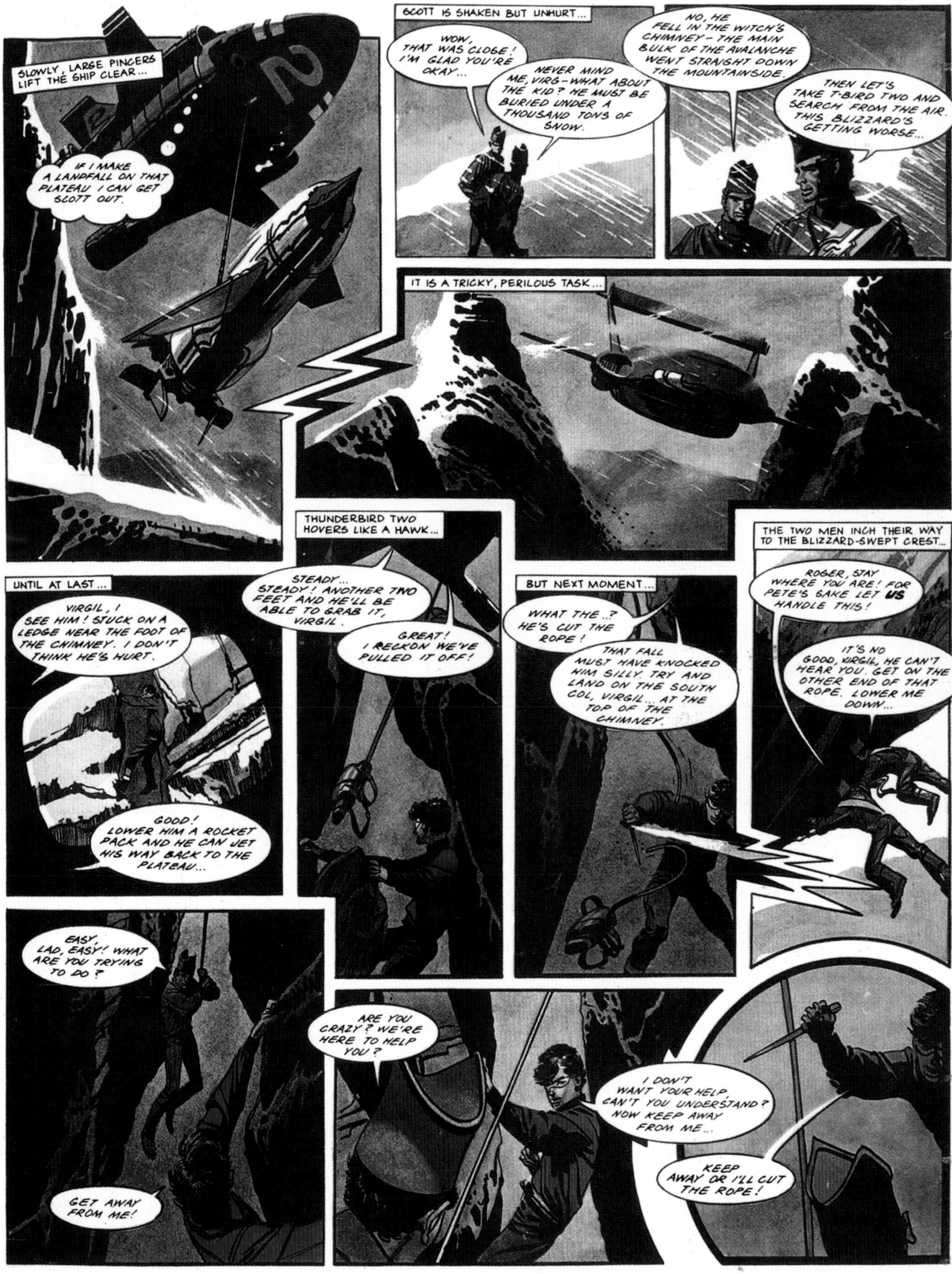
SLOWLY, LARGE PINCERS LIFT THE SHIP CLEAR...
IF I MAKE A LANDFALL ON THAT PLATEAU I CAN GET SCOTT OUT.
SCOTT IS SHAKEN BUT UNHURT...
WOW, THAT WAS CLOSE! I'M GLAD YOU'RE OKAY...
NEVER MIND ME, VIRG - WHAT ABOUT THE KID? HE MUST BE BURIED UNDER A THOUSAND TONS OF SNOW.
NO, HE FELL IN THE WITCH'S CHIMNEY - THE MAIN BULK OF THE AVALANCHE WENT STRAIGHT DOWN THE MOUNTAINSIDE.
THEN LET'S TAKE T-BIRD TWO AND SEARCH FROM THE AIR. THIS BLIZZARD'S GETTING WORSE...
IT IS A TRICKY, PERILOUS TASK...
UNTIL AT LAST...
VIRGIL, I SEE HIM! STUCK ON A LEDGE NEAR THE FOOT OF THE CHIMNEY. I DON'T THINK HE'S HURT.
GOOD! LOWER HIM A ROCKET PACK AND HE CAN JET HIS WAY BACK TO THE PLATEAU...
THUNDERBIRD TWO HOVERS LIKE A HAWK...
STEADY... STEADY! ANOTHER TWO FEET AND HE'LL BE ABLE TO GRAB IT, VIRGIL.
GREAT! I RECKON WE'VE PULLED IT OFF!
BUT NEXT MOMENT...
WHAT THE ..? HE'S CUT THE ROPE!
THAT FALL MUST HAVE KNOCKED HIM SILLY. TRY AND LAND ON THE SOUTH COL, VIRGIL... AT THE TOP OF THE CHIMNEY.
THE TWO MEN INCH THEIR WAY TO THE BLIZZARD-SWEPT CREST...
ROGER, STAY WHERE YOU ARE! FOR PETE'S SAKE LET US HANDLE THIS!
IT'S NO GOOD, VIRGIL, HE CAN'T HEAR YOU. GET ON THE OTHER END OF THAT ROPE. LOWER ME DOWN...
EASY, LAD, EASY! WHAT ARE YOU TRYING TO DO?
GET AWAY FROM ME!
ARE YOU CRAZY? WE'RE HERE TO HELP YOU?
I DON'T WANT YOUR HELP. CAN'T YOU UNDERSTAND? NOW KEEP AWAY FROM ME...
KEEP AWAY OR I'LL CUT THE ROPE!

Part 3 - dateline 10 August 2068

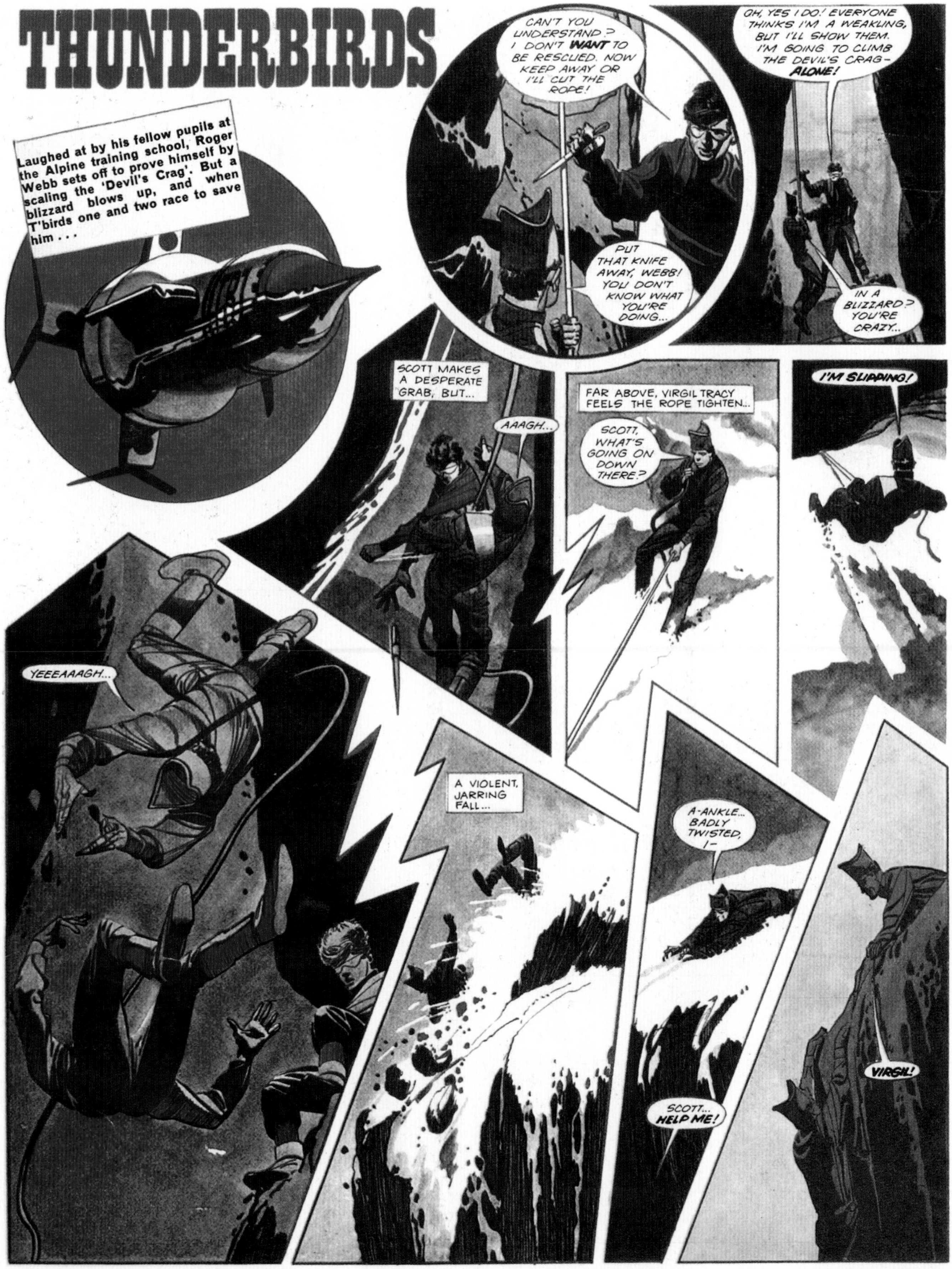
THUNDERBIRDS
Laughed at by his fellow pupils at the Alpine training school, Roger Webb sets off to prove himself by scaling the 'Devil's Crag'. But a blizzard blows up, and when T'birds one and two race to save him . . .
CAN'T YOU UNDERSTAND? I DON'T WANT TO BE RESCUED. NOW KEEP AWAY OR I'LL CUT THE ROPE!
PUT THAT KNIFE AWAY, WEBB! YOU DON'T KNOW WHAT YOU'RE DOING...
OH, YES I DO! EVERYONE THINKS I'M A WEAKLING, BUT I'LL SHOW THEM. I'M GOING TO CLIMB THE DEVIL'S CRAG - ALONE!
IN A BLIZZARD? YOU'RE CRAZY...
SCOTT MAKES A DESPERATE GRAB, BUT...
AAAGH...
FAR ABOVE, VIRGIL TRACY FEELS THE ROPE TIGHTEN...
SCOTT, WHAT'S GOING ON DOWN THERE?
I'M SLIPPING!
YEEEAAAGH...
A VIOLENT, JARRING FALL...
A-ANKLE... BADLY TWISTED, I-
SCOTT... HELP ME!
VIRGIL!

Artist: Frank Bellamy

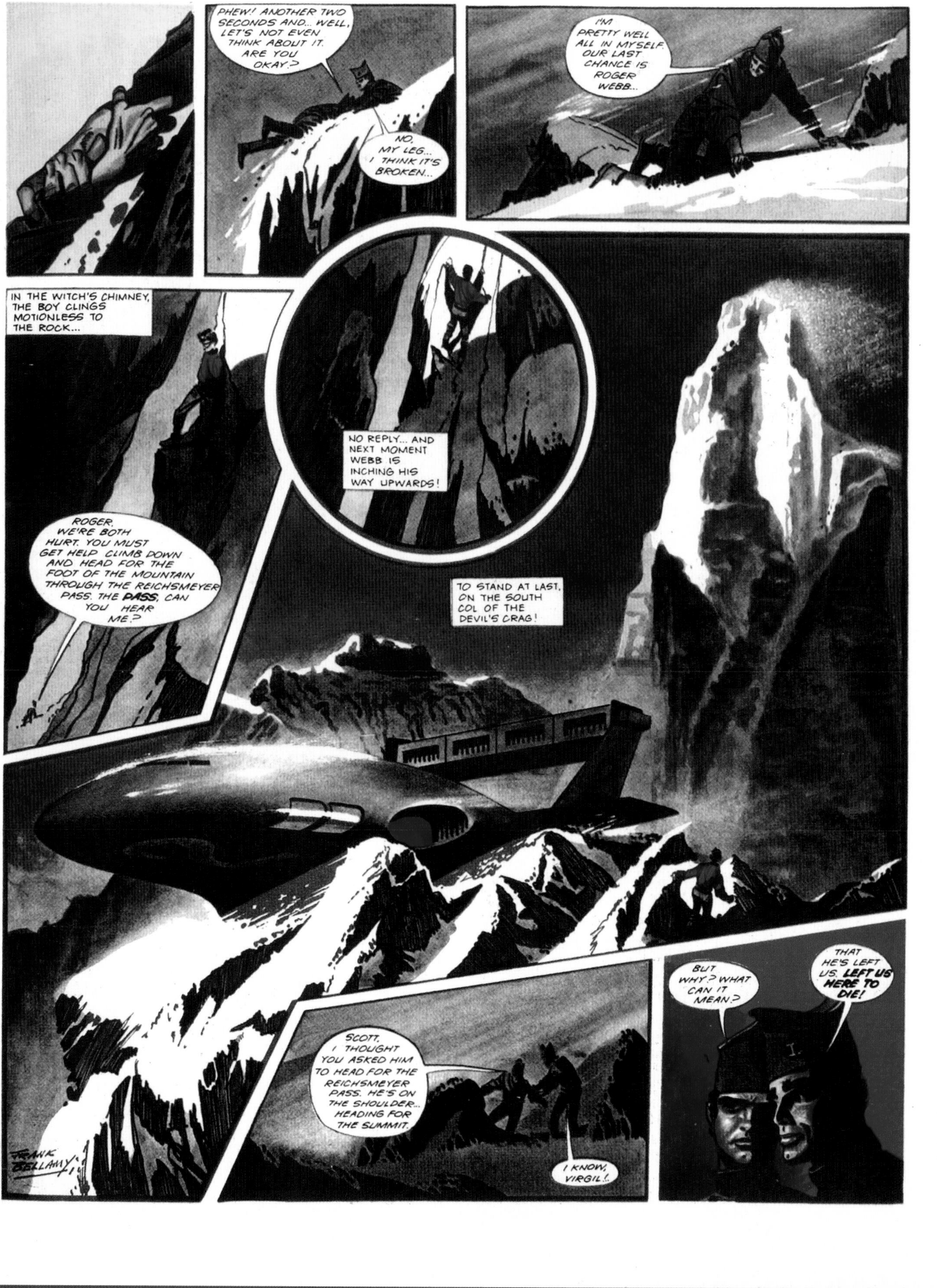
PHEW! ANOTHER TWO SECONDS AND... WELL, LET'S NOT EVEN THINK ABOUT IT. ARE YOU OKAY?
NO, MY LEG... I THINK IT'S BROKEN...
I'M PRETTY WELL ALL IN MYSELF. OUR LAST CHANCE IS ROGER WEBB...
IN THE WITCH'S CHIMNEY, THE BOY CLINGS MOTIONLESS TO THE ROCK...
ROGER, WE'RE BOTH HURT. YOU MUST GET HELP. CLIMB DOWN AND HEAD FOR THE FOOT OF THE MOUNTAIN THROUGH THE REICHSMEYER PASS. THE PASS, CAN YOU HEAR ME?
NO REPLY... AND NEXT MOMENT WEBB IS INCHING HIS WAY UPWARDS!
TO STAND AT LAST, ON THE SOUTH COL OF THE DEVIL'S CRAG!
FRANK BELLAMY
SCOTT, I THOUGHT YOU ASKED HIM TO HEAD FOR THE REICHSMEYER PASS. HE'S ON THE SHOULDER... HEADING FOR THE SUMMIT.
I KNOW, VIRGIL!
BUT WHY? WHAT CAN IT MEAN?
THAT HE'S LEFT US. LEFT US HERE TO DIE!

Part 4 - dateline 17 August 2068

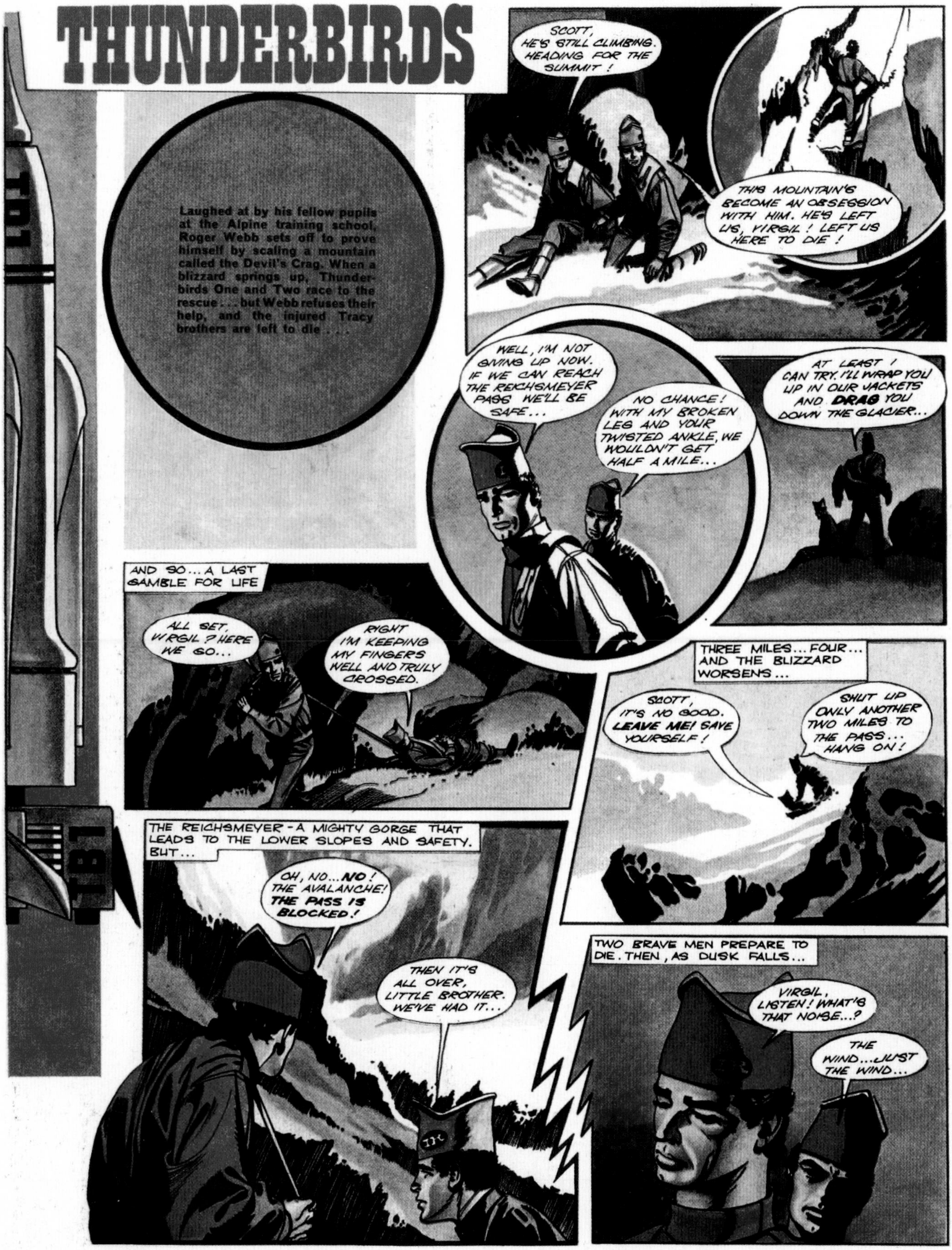
THUNDERBIRDS
Laughed at by his fellow pupils at the Alpine training school, Roger Webb sets off to prove himself by scaling a mountain called the Devil's Crag. When a blizzard springs up, Thunderbirds One and Two race to the rescue . . . but Webb refuses their help, and the injured Tracy brothers are left to die . . .
SCOTT, HE'S STILL CLIMBING. HEADING FOR THE SUMMIT!
THIS MOUNTAIN'S BECOME AN OBSESSION WITH HIM. HE'S LEFT US, VIRGIL! LEFT US HERE TO DIE!
WELL, I'M NOT GIVING UP NOW. IF WE CAN REACH THE REICHSMEYER PASS WE'LL BE SAFE...
NO CHANCE! WITH MY BROKEN LEG AND YOUR TWISTED ANKLE, WE WOULDN'T GET HALF A MILE...
AT LEAST I CAN TRY. I'LL WRAP YOU UP IN OUR JACKETS AND DRAG YOU DOWN THE GLACIER...
AND SO... A LAST GAMBLE FOR LIFE
ALL SET, VIRGIL? HERE WE GO...
RIGHT I'M KEEPING MY FINGERS WELL AND TRULY CROSSED.
THREE MILES... FOUR... AND THE BLIZZARD WORSENS...
SCOTT, IT'S NO GOOD. LEAVE ME! SAVE YOURSELF!
SHUT UP ONLY ANOTHER TWO MILES TO THE PASS... HANG ON!
THE REICHSMEYER - A MIGHTY GORGE THAT LEADS TO THE LOWER SLOPES AND SAFETY. BUT...
OH, NO... NO! THE AVALANCHE! THE PASS IS BLOCKED!
THEN IT'S ALL OVER, LITTLE BROTHER. WE'VE HAD IT...
TWO BRAVE MEN PREPARE TO DIE. THEN, AS DUSK FALLS...
VIRGIL, LISTEN! WHAT'S THAT NOISE...?
THE WIND... JUST THE WIND...

Artist: Frank Bellamy

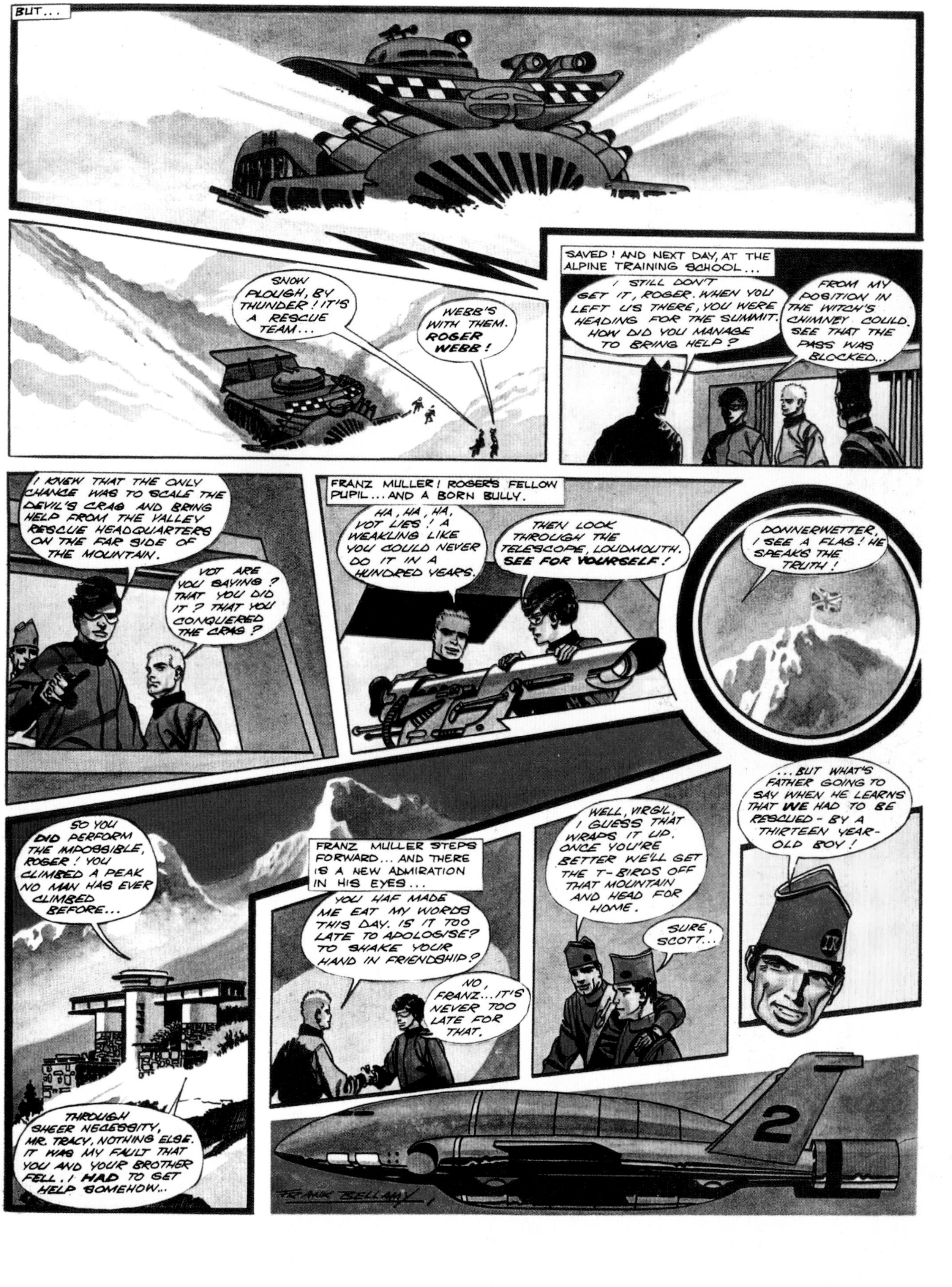
BUT...
SNOW PLOUGH, BY THUNDER! IT'S A RESCUE TEAM...
WEBB'S WITH THEM. ROGER WEBB!
SAVED! AND NEXT DAY, AT THE ALPINE TRAINING SCHOOL...
I STILL DON'T GET IT, ROGER. WHEN YOU LEFT US THERE, YOU WERE HEADING FOR THE SUMMIT. HOW DID YOU MANAGE TO BRING HELP?
FROM MY POSITION IN THE WITCH'S CHIMNEY COULD SEE THAT THE PASS WAS BLOCKED...
I KNEW THAT THE ONLY CHANCE WAS TO SCALE THE DEVIL'S CRAG AND BRING HELP FROM THE VALLEY RESCUE HEADQUARTERS ON THE FAR SIDE OF THE MOUNTAIN.
VOT ARE YOU SAYING? THAT YOU DID IT? THAT YOU CONQUERED THE CRAG?
FRANZ MULLER! ROGER'S FELLOW PUPIL... AND A BORN BULLY.
HA, HA, HA, VOT LIES! A WEAKLING LIKE YOU COULD NEVER DO IT IN A HUNDRED YEARS.
THEN LOOK THROUGH THE TELESCOPE, LOUDMOUTH. SEE FOR YOURSELF!
DONNERWETTER, I SEE A FLAG! HE SPEAKS THE TRUTH!
SO YOU DID PERFORM THE IMPOSSIBLE, ROGER! YOU CLIMBED A PEAK NO MAN HAS EVER CLIMBED BEFORE...
THROUGH SHEER NECESSITY, MR. TRACY, NOTHING ELSE. IT WAS MY FAULT THAT YOU AND YOUR BROTHER FELL. I HAD TO GET HELP SOMEHOW...
FRANZ MULLER STEPS FORWARD... AND THERE IS A NEW ADMIRATION IN HIS EYES...
YOU HAF MADE ME EAT MY WORDS THIS DAY. IS IT TOO LATE TO APOLOGISE? TO SHAKE YOUR HAND IN FRIENDSHIP?
NO, FRANZ... IT'S NEVER TOO LATE FOR THAT.
WELL, VIRGIL, I GUESS THAT WRAPS IT UP. ONCE YOU'RE BETTER WE'LL GET THE T-BIRDS OFF THAT MOUNTAIN AND HEAD FOR HOME.
SURE, SCOTT...
...BUT WHAT'S FATHER GOING TO SAY WHEN HE LEARNS THAT WE HAD TO BE RESCUED - BY A THIRTEEN YEAR-OLD BOY!
2
FRANK BELLAMY

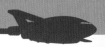

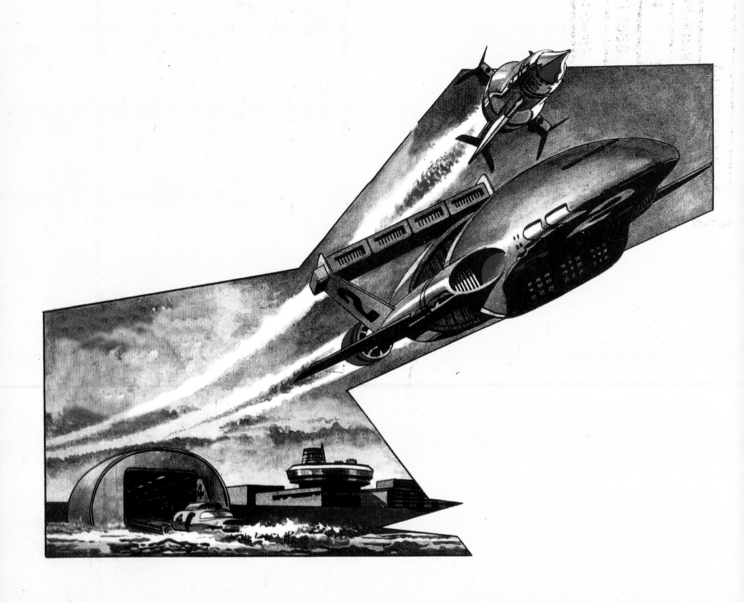

CLASSIC
COMICS

EGMONT